Superstocks

Superstocks

A New Method To Uncover
Rapid Appreciation Stocks

by Hugh Ferguson

Windsor Books, Brightwaters, N.Y.

Copyright 1979 by Hugh Ferguson
All rights reserved
This book, or parts thereof,
may not be reproduced in any form without the
permission of the publishers.

Published by Windsor Books
P.O. Box 280
Brightwaters, N.Y., 11718

Manufactured in the United States of America

CAVEAT: It should be noted that all securities, charts, formulas, systems or other devices discussed in this book are for illustrative purposes only and are not to be construed as specific recommendations, directly or indirectly, as to which securities to buy or sell, or when to buy or sell them; or that any method of investing is foolproof or without difficulty. All ideas presented are entirely those of the author(s), and do not necessarily reflect those of the publisher or bookseller.

TABLE OF CONTENTS

1. **Stock Market Players Anonymous—
   Or Is The Market For You?**..........................11
   - Why some people actually want to lose money.
   - Why Americans are prone to suicide.
   - How to judge if you're self-destructive.

2. **Playing Jean Dixon With The Market—
   Or Are We Bullish Or Bearish?**......................17
   - What is the "scientific method."
   - The Federal Government's scientific method.
   - Where to find the figures for the economic indicators.
   - What the economic indicators mean.
   - The 12 leading indicators.
   - How to use the leading indicators.
   - In a nutshell.

3. **Companies With Financial Muscle—
   Or How To Pick Growth Stocks**......................31
   - Why stock prices change.
   - Why growth stocks should be bought.
   - My definition of a growth stock.
   - Where to find growth stocks.
   - How to use the Standard and Poor's stock reports.
   - Watch those quarterly earnings.
   - In a nutshell.
   - When to hop back on the growth company.
   - In a nutshell.
   - Don't worry about price-earnings ratios.

4. **The Key To The Vault—
   Or When To Buy And Sell Each Growth Stock** 47
   - What is meant by the technical aspect of the market.
   - The point and figure method.
   - The daily bar chart.
   - Moving averages.
   - The Elliott Wave Theory.
   - The relative strength concept.
   - Don Worden's "tick volume."
   - The configurations of Edwards and Magee.
   - My own weekly minor trend rules.
   - Illustrations of the minor trend rule.

5. **Play It Again, Sam—
   Or Let's See If You Can Do It** 85
   - Work sheets and figures.

6. **Etcetera, Etcetera, Etcetera—
   Or How To Track Additional Growth Stocks** 105
   - Some illustrations.
   - How to buy a growth oriented mutual fund.

7. **For Mathematicians Only—
   Or How To Pick A Growth Stock That's Undervalued** 127
   - The importance of mathematics.
   - Why mathematics is used in stock analysis.
   - The mathematics of compound interest.
   - Applying the mathematics of growth.
   - A valuable short-cut.
   - A short-cut of a short-cut.

8 **The Devil Theory—
   Buy On Breaks, Sell On Rallies** 149
   - The devil in past times.
   - The devil in modern garb.
   - The devils of Wall Street.
   - How to take advantage of the devil.

9. **Turning Disasters Into Profits—Or Buying The Industry Group With The Most Potential** **159**
   - The bear market of 1960 and profits.
   - The bear market of 1962 and profits.
   - The bear market of 1966 and profits.
   - The bear market of 1969 and profits.
   - Illustrations from the 1970 bear market and the ensuing bull market.
   - An illustration from the 1973-4 bear market.

10. **Let The Yellow Pages Do Your Walking— Or How To Pick the Strongest Stocks**.................**181**
    - What relative strength is.
    - The tools you'll need—and how to use them.

11. **How To Buy "Grade A" Growth Companies— And Milk Them For Profits**.......................**185**
    - What is meant by quality growth stocks.
    - How quality was used at the beginning of the bull market.
    - How to find the quality growth companies.
    - Finding new quality growth companies.

12. **Although There's No Warranty When You Buy Warrants—Sometimes They Warrant Your Buying Them**....................................**193**
    - The yo-yo characteristics of warrants.
    - A useful analogy.
    - What a warrant is.
    - How the price of a warrant is set.
    - Only two rules are needed to buy warrants.

13. **How To Trade Safely and Almost For Nothing**.........**203**
    - Prologue of some sophisticated techniques.
    - Call options.
    - Deep discount bonds.
    - The "short" sale.
    - Putting it all to work.

14. **The "Have Your Cake And Eat It Too" Security........217**
    - All about convertible bonds.
    - Where to find out if a growth company has a convertible.
    - The reading, writing, and arithmetic of convertibles.
    - Figuring the premium.

15. **Expect The Unexpected—
    Go Short Of The Market While You're Long...........247**
    - How the unexpected paid off.
    - Applying the unexpected to the stock market.
    - Why the convertible bond hedge works.
    - More about a "short" sale.
    - Eye-opener illustrations.
    - Double your pleasure, double your profits.

16. **The Track Of The Bear—
    Or How To Act In A Down Market....................233**
    - The cyclical nature of nature.
    - The cyclical nature of man's institutions.
    - Signs of the end of a bull market.
    - Using the same techniques to go short in a bear market.

ILLUSTRATIONS

1. Leading Indicators...............................28
1a. Leading Indicators As Published
    In The Wall Street Journal.........................29
2a. Houston Natural Gas..............................38
2b. Houston Natural Gas..............................39
3. Elliot Bull Market 56
4. Allied Stores......................................65
5. Ametek 70
6. Bendix..75
7. Bordens 80
8. Tyler Corp 91
9. Universal Leaf Tobacco............................96
10. Olin Corp 107
11. Super Value 110
12. Abbott Labs 114
13. Church's Fried Chicken 118
14. Datapoint Corp...................................122
15. Price (Rowe) Growth 125
16. Gulf And Western 214
17. Rite Aid...253

9

CHAPTER 1

STOCK MARKET PLAYERS ANONYMOUS—
Or Is The Market For You?

WHY SOME PEOPLE ACTUALLY
WANT TO LOSE MONEY

I'm sure that it is no secret to a few of you, but it will be a great shock to most of you, that there are actually some people who *want* to lose money in the stock market.

These players won't admit it, but they don't want to make any profits. They love the action and excitement, and it does make for fascinating barroom, athletic club or golf-playing talk.

Arnold is a man over 50. His children are on the road to success, while his wife is happily engaged in social activities. He has plenty of money as the result of an inheritance and the sale of his father's business. He just doesn't like golf or tennis, the dogs or horses. His

Stock Market Players Anonymous

pleasure is trading stocks.

Why not? The board room has comfortable chairs, is climate controlled, charges no admissions, and is where the action is. It's easy to become a tape watcher and plunk down your bet not once, but several times a day.

Arnold has convinced himself he's not gambling, but investing. This is a business like the one he just sold. His broker loves it, because the more Arnold trades, the greater the broker's "comish."

Before you consider the skeleton and flesh of this book, it is imperative that you look in the mirror to see if you blush. Are you another Arnold? Should you join an organization that might be called "Stock Market Players Anonymous?"

It may be worthwhile for you to have some insight into the reasons why some Americans turn to drugs and drinking and gambling. I believe that these are but forms of suicide, although they are excruciatingly slow and premeditated. After all, taking the gas pipe or shooting a bullet through the brain is faster.

Those who are religious should have no trouble in thinking that a person has a body and a soul. In fact, the great majority of the world's population probably accepts this. If you were brought up in the East as Brahman or Buddhist, you would be convinced that the body is only a dwelling place for the soul and can be abandoned at will by the owner. Therefore, if you were playing the modern Japanese stock market in Tokyo and suffered severe losses, you could, in good conscience, run a sword through your stomach. By flinging your body on the garbage heap, your soul would be free. Your Oriental friends and

Stock Market Players Anonymous

relatives would readily accept this as an honorable deed.

But an American who wants to escape the consequences has an extremely difficult job in killing his body. All of the religious, cultural, legal and educational patterns are dead set against it. If he kills himself, he might not even get a decent burial. Any American contemplating suicide should make sure he can succeed. If he fails, he will be punished for a crime. It's a case of, "you're damned if you do and damned if you don't."

Suicides occur mostly among those who have a great deal and those who have very little. The wealthy and the poor are prime candidates. Since the poor, by definition, have no money with which to play the market, we'll concentrate on the wealthy.

Suicide seems to be endemic in those societies which place emphasis on individuality. It makes no difference whether they are primitive or sophisticated. Where you find people constantly clawing for power, scrounging for the buck, or hustling for success, you will find the highest suicide rate.

WHY AMERICANS ARE PRONE TO SUICIDE

Americans are ideal candidates. We live in a pressure cooker. The ethos of our culture sings its siren song of success and we try to dance to its tune. If we are out of step, however, we cannot behead ourselves—we cannot commit suicide by destroying our bodies.

Instead, we reverse the Oriental philosophy. We do not kill our bodies to release our souls; we destroy our souls so

Stock Market Players Anonymous

that our bodies become shells. The objective is the same, only the means have changed.

HOW TO JUDGE IF YOU'RE SELF-DESTRUCTIVE

Before continuing with the rest of this book, it is important that you recognize any self-destructive tendencies. The following questions are those asked by Gamblers Anonymous. The phrases "investing" or "playing the market" have been substituted for "gambling" in their standard list of 20 questions. If you answer "yes" to at least seven you are in need of help to stay away from the market.

1. Do you take time off from work to play the market? This includes not only absenting yourself physically by being at the brokerage house, but also by using working hours for frequent phone calls. For women it means leaving the house chores and neglecting the children.

2. Is investing making your life unhappy?

3. Is investing affecting your reputation? Are you so tied up with the market that your professional competence is lessening?

4. Have you ever felt remorse after a bout with the market? Do you feel plain lousy because of the guilt feelings?

5. Do you play the market to get money with which to pay debts?

6. Does investing cause a decrease in your ambition?

7. After losing money in investments, do you feel you must reinvest as soon as possible to win back your losses?

Stock Market Players Anonymous

8. After making a profit, do you have a strong urge to try to make more?
9. Do you often play the market until you're broke?
10. Do you ever borrow to finance your market playing?
11. Have you ever sold any real estate or personal property to play the market?
12. Are you reluctant to use investment money for normal expenditures?
13. Does playing the market make you careless of your family's welfare?
14. Do you ever play the market for more money than you planned?
15. Do you ever play the market to escape worry or trouble?
16. Have you ever committed or considered committing an illegal act to finance your market activities?
17. Do your investments create difficulty in sleeping?
18. Do arguments, disappointments or frustrations give you an urge to play the market?
19. Do you want to celebrate any good fortune by playing the market?
20. Have you ever considered suicide or other forms of slow self-destruction (drugs, alcohol) as a result of your investments?

Remember, if you answer "yes" to at least seven of these, you are in need of help. You may need to join "Stock Market Players Anonymous!"

CHAPTER 2

PLAYING JEAN DIXON WITH THE MARKET—
Or Are We Bullish Or Bearish?

There are supposed to be some people who have supernatural gifts; they can somehow see into the future better than others. These powers may be due to God, to a serendipity of the genes, or to the ingestion of certain of nature's foods. The predictive powers of these individuals take the communicative forms of astrology, Egyptology, biblical mysteries, phrenology, tea leaf reading and spell casting.

That's fine for the "gifted" seers and their followers, but what can the rest of us do? Simply this—we're going to follow the same cultural evolution that Western man used to up-lift himself from the superstition of witchcraft and slavery to the present day enlightenment of Women's Lib and footprints on the moon. We are going to use the "scientific method" as applied to the stock market.

Playing Jean Dixon With The Market

WHAT IS THE SCIENTIFIC METHOD?

The "scientific method"—it really should be "methods"—is that which we apply every day in our lives. There is no secret to it. It is simply making a rule from observed "facts" and seeing if that rule works in the future. If it doesn't, then we just make a new rule to include what did work before and try it all over again. This is a system of trial and error that continues until as many errors as possible are eliminated. I suppose it can be called "monkey effort"—but with intelligence.

THE FEDERAL GOVERNMENT'S SCIENTIFIC METHOD

Fortunately for us, we have such a "scientific method" for the market. It's been all worked out for us with our tax dollars. This is one time we're going to get something valuable from Uncle Sam. The Department of Commerce has spent millions of dollars, twirled thousands of dials, and filled buckets of sweat trying to figure out what makes business boom or bust.

Government and private economists have compiled and digested all of the vital facts concerning all of the nation's business cycles going back to 1854. This date apparently marks the culmination of a number of very important inventions that finally changed America from an agricultural country to an industrial giant. A brief history would be informative, and possibly helpful.

Playing Jean Dixon With The Market

Keep in mind that we were once English colonies, just as South Africa, India, and a host of other populated real estate was. In 1774, the English Parliament was persuaded by powerful British manufacturers and merchants to pass laws to prevent not only machines from leaving the country, but the plans and drawings of machines as well. Since the English were among the first of the world powers to swing into the Industrial Revolution, they naturally wanted to keep all the rewards for themselves.

But one thing you simply cannot legislate out of existence is the human mind. In 1790 an English waver named Sam Slater came to the United States with a pretty complete knowledge of weaving and of the machines used. This jackal had worked since he was fourteen as an apprentice at one of England's leading textile factories. Sam no sooner landed in New York, when he heard of the great difficulties someone was having up in New England trying to put together a textile plant. So he went to Moses Brown in Rhode Island, and built from memory the textile machines that carded and spun. Within a year, Sam had the first successful cotton mill in America—starting this country's Industrial Revolution.

Slater's mill started the cotton ball rolling. Sam wasn't the only one with a memory. As mechanics came and went from the old factory in Pawtucket, they carried the plans for machinery all over New England. New mills were opening like barrooms after Prohibition. A great demand went up for more and more cotton.

The trouble was there wasn't enough cotton. The only source was from the South, but this variety was very hard to clean. One slave working one whole day could clean seeds from only about one pound of cotton. The solution came from a very unlikely source—a school teacher who never taught.

Eli Whitney, after graduating from Yale, took a job as a teacher in a small Southern town. On the way, he stopped off at a cotton plantation and heard the owners yapping about how much money they could make from selling cotton to the New England mills if they could only get the dad-blasted seeds out. While Eli was thinking about this conversation, he suddenly had a flash as to how to do it. In ten days, he made a model that worked. With it, Eli and a horse were able to do the ginning of fifty men. The cotton gin was the second spoke in America's wheel.

Sam Slater now had plenty of cotton to spin into yarn. In the meantime, the lack of power weaving looms was holding back the manufacture of yarn into cloth. Most of the weaving was still done by hand and, what was a weaver to do?

So the Americans pulled another Sam Slater. They went to England and memorized how an English power loom was put together. One of these was Francis Lowell, who supposedly went to England for his health. He did, indeed, and came back much healthier financially. For Francis did build the first successful power loom in this country. His efforts caused the price of cotton cloth to drop from 33 cents to 10 cents a yard. Thus, cotton manufacturing became the first great American industry.

Whitney made the cotton, Slater the yarn, Lowell the cloth. But the seamstresses and tailors still had to sew by hand. What if someone could figure out a way to join the cloth? This was done by Elias Howe in 1845. Elias and his

Playing Jean Dixon With The Market

machine entered a contest against five expert seamstresses. The crowd gasped as his machine did 200 stitches a minute against their 30. Imagine a man beating five women at sewing!

So here we have the first complete industry—from raw cotton to the sewn garment.

The next great stride forward came from standardization of parts and, subsequently their mass production. This was especially true in the sewing machine industry under Isaac Singer, and the gun and rifle industry under Eli Whitney and Sam Colt.

Rubber was the next important spoke for the industrial wheel. The word comes from Priestly, an English chemist who experimented with the gummed balls that came from the New World. He picked up a ball of gum one day and discovered it would erase pencil marks. He was so flabbergasted that he cut up the ball into pieces and sent them to his friends. He called the pieces "rubbers," since they rubbed out the marks. That was in 1770.

About 1820, a Boston ship captain brought home from South America (as a gift to a friend) a pair of rubber shoes. A little later, 500 pairs were imported and sold. Some merchants began to import the rubber to manufacture their own shoes. From there, they made rubber clothing.

Early experiments with rubber attempted to make imitation black leather. Turpentine was mixed with lampblack and rubber and spread on cloth. But the stuff melted and smelled badly in the heat of summer and became brittle and stiff in the cold of winter.

Then along came Charles Goodyear. He worked fruit-

Playing Jean Dixon With The Market

lessly for years trying to improve the properties of rubber. One day in 1839, he accidentally dropped some rubber mixed with sulfur on a hot stove—result, Vulcanized rubber.

In agriculture, the plough was greatly improved. Huge amounts of soil could be planted, but the harvesting was agonizing. Grasses (grains) were hand cut with a sickle until Cyrus McCormick developed the first American reaper in 1831.

After 1830, it was becoming clearer to American businessmen that the greatest need in industry was steel. Railroad builders, machine-shop owners, fire-arm manufacturers, everyone wanted cheap steel. Finally, in 1846, Bill Kelly invented a new iron making machine, one that blew huge amounts of air into the iron in the furnace, which burned out all the impurities. (In England, a similar process was invented by Henry Bessemer so that all of these furnaces are known as the "Bessemer" process for making steel).

So there you have, very briefly, the on-rush of inventions and the development of American Industry culminating in the first boom and bust, with the business cycle studied in 1854.

What have the federal and private economists come up with? Plenty! They have found statistical measurements, called indicators, that lag the business cycle, those that go step-in-step with it, and those which lead it. Massive and monumental work was undertaken by Wesley Mitchell and Art Burns, the first head of Eisenhower's Council of Economic Advisors. It was continued by Goeffrey Moore whose staff combed through more than 800 statistical

Playing Jean Dixon With The Market

series before they came up with a few that lead the business cycle.

WHERE TO FIND THE FIGURES FOR THE ECONOMIC INDICATORS

All these important economic indicators and the records of each since World War II can be obtained from the U.S. Government printing office in Washington, D.C. This valuable publication is called "Business Conditions Digest."

If you don't want to spend the money for it, you can follow their course in any paper with a good financial section. Every month a summary is published that makes headlines. Later on you'll see how you can keep your own simple chart based on the Government statistics so you won't have to rely on anyone.

WHAT THE ECONOMIC INDICATORS MEAN

Suppose that you read that plant and equipment spending is rising. That ought to be bullish news. But, alas, that's a lagging indicator. This usually shows strength when the recovery is well along.

Or, perhaps you hear on TV that more people are going to work, that jobs are opening up, that the kids graduating are finding jobs. Don't be too happy. This is a coincident indicator. It moves with the business cycle and doesn't help us in our forecasting.

Playing Jean Dixon With the Market

How about the great news that consumer prices are going down. Chops and canned peaches and milk are dropping. It seems that inflation is getting under control. Will this help us figure the future? Sorry, the answer is no. For this is just another indicator that stays in step, like a dancing partner, with business conditions.

Certainly, a going over of the help-wanted section should be useful. With more jobs looking for workers, with unemployment being lowered, we should be able to forecast. Not so; this is just another coincident statistic.

A great store is put into consumer spending plans. The University of Michigan, as well as the government and others, are always trying to gauge the purposes of consumers. Are they thinking of buying more cars, refrigerators, houses, or widgits? If the thought is father to the deed, then this certainly should help us. Unfortunately, it doesn't. The researchers have empirically determined that consumer spending plans only go hand in hand with the business cycle.

Well, then, where do we go from here? To those indicators that tell us what trend lies *ahead*. The business cycle is generally pictured as having periods of expanding economic activity followed by periods of contracting economic activity. These activities include total production, employment, income, consumption, trade and the flow of funds.

Since 1938, the National Bureau of Economic Analysis has maintained a list of cyclical indicators which are called leaders, coinciders or laggers in relation to the movement of the business cycle. The most recent list was revised in 1966.

Playing Jean Dixon With The Market

The Bureau has a long list of 78 cyclical indicators and a short list drawn from these which provide a convenient summary of the current situation. This short list consists of 26 series: 12 leading, 8 coincident, and 6 lagging. It is the 12 leading indicators we are most concerned with. They are tabulated below.

THE 12 LEADING INDICATORS

1. The average workweek of production workers in manufacturing.
2. The net number of business formations. (That is, the difference between the new businesses formed and the old ones that went out of business).
3. Index of stock prices, 500 common stocks. (Notice this is the broad list from the Standard and Poor Index and not the 30 industrials that make up the Dow Jones Index).
4. The number of new housing building permits.
5. The layoff rate in manufacturing.
6. The new orders, consumer goods and materials, in 1967 dollars.
7. Contracts and orders for plant and equipment, in 1967 dollars.
8. The net change in inventories on hand and on order in 1967 dollars.
9. The percent of change in sensitive prices. This is a list of crude materials and does not include foods or feeds.
10. Vendor performance or the percent of companies reporting slower deliveries.
11. The money balance, M1, in 1967 dollars. (These are

demand deposits and checking accounts).

12. The percent of change in total liquid assets. (This is a measure of the changes in the wealth held in liquid form by private nonfinancial advisors).

Let's see why these particular indicators should move ahead of business as a whole.

If more new businesses are being formed. (#2), then the risk-takers smell that something is up. It takes a lot of guts to put money, time and energy on the line hoping to make a profit. So the number of new businesses is an excellent leading indicator.

Once the decision to start a business has been made, a plant and equipment has to be ordered (#7). The new employees decrease the layoff rate (#5).

Employees need new housing (#4).

The new firms create a demand for building up inventories by the already established firms (#8).

As industry hums and more orders pour in two things happen: the average workweek of manufacturing employees increases (#1), and companies have trouble getting out their deliveries on time (#10).

As mentioned above there are new orders for all kinds of things: consumer goods and materials (#6).

Crude materials such as copper, coal, oil, gas, etc., move up in price because of shortages (#9).

The change in the money supply is very important. It consists of M1 and M2. M1 is the total of private demand and equals the total in checking accounts, deposits and cash in the hands of the public. They represent funds most easily available for spending (#11). Better business leads to a more favorable attitude and thus money is spent more

Playing Jean Dixon With The Market

freely in all sectors of the economy. The change in total liquid assets is part of the money supply (#12). Whereas the money supply, M1, shows the quantity of private wealth at each reading, this indicator measures the changes in wealth. The first is a static figure, the second is the rate of change of those figures.

The last of the indicators is the index of stock prices (#3). This one is interesting because it acts as a kind of thermometer telling us the heat being generated in the faster moving economy. Once a trend gets going, it will continue until the whole process reverses.

HOW TO USE THE LEADING INDICATORS

According to the government, if, after the leading indicators have been heading down for some months, they turn up for three consecutive months, then we are out of the recession and the economy will continue to improve. If you look on the chart of the leading indicators, you will see such a turn in May of 1975. For that reason, all of our buy signals on our growth companies came at the end of May, 1975.

On the other hand, when we get three months of decreasing figures, we are in a recession. That is the date we will sell (go short) a growth stock that has stopped growing.

As you can see from the chart (Figure 1, which is a blow-up of part of the chart of Figure 1a), we got such a sell signal in October of 1973. In the chapter on short selling you will see how well we made out on the short sale of Rite Aid.

FIGURE 1: Leading Indicators

Leading Indicators

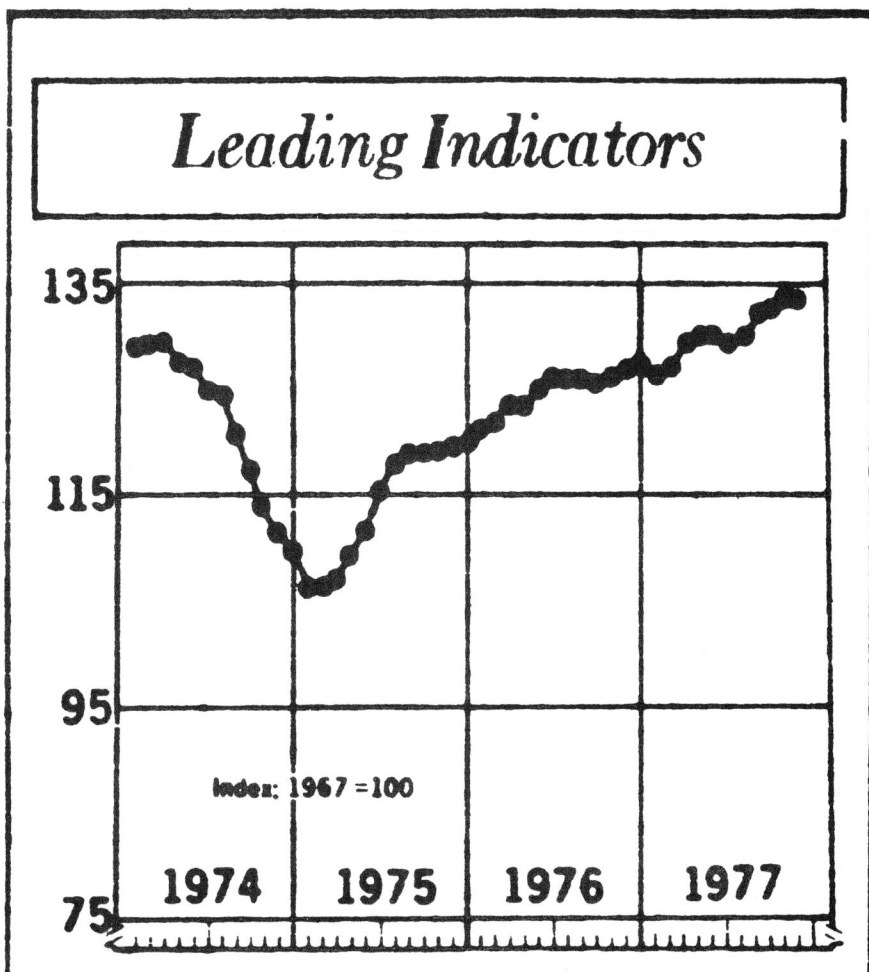

COMPOSITE of key indicators of future economic activity fell in November to 133.8% of the 1967 average from a revised 134.8% in October, the Commerce Department reports. (See story on page 2.)

FIGURE 1a:
Leading Indicators As Published in the Wall Street Journal [1974-1977]
Source: **Wall Street Journal**, Dow Jones & Co., Inc.

Playing Jean Dixon With The Market

IN A NUTSHELL

It is not necessary to have occult powers or to play Jean Dixon in order to figure out whether the market is bullish or bearish. The Federal Government does it for you. In fact, the Wall Street Journal even prints the chart on the front page every month (Figure 1a). By following these leading indicators, you will be able to be your own "swami" and predict the future course of the stock market.

CHAPTER 3

COMPANIES WITH FINANCIAL MUSCLE—
Or How To Pick Growth Stocks

The average investor is under several misapprehensions about stocks. One is that the money paid for a stock he just bought goes into the coffers of that company. It does nothing of the sort unless the stock is a new issue or a secondary offering. All buying and selling is between old owners and new owners with no money going to the company. All that happens is that a piece of paper representing ownership changes hands.

This brings up the most fundamental question in the field of investments. Why should you buy a piece of ownership called a stock certificate? To put it another way, can you sell it to another party at a higher price and thereby make a profit? Why should the price of a stock increase anyway? This is like asking questions that are basic in religion. Is there a God? What is God? Can I

Companies With Financial Muscle

benefit by believing in God? In the physical sciences, there are also such basic questions. The physicists find, after peeling matter back layer by layer like onion skins, that there is hardly anything left but mathematical formulae. They are driven continuously to ask the basic questions: What is matter? What is energy? What is gravity?

WHY STOCK PRICES CHANGE

Every field of study has its basic questions and temporary fluid changing answers. (Sometimes even the questions change, but this takes longer). The answer to our basic question, "What makes the price of a stock increase?," seems to me to be like this. Take a rather simple situation: all things being equal, you would put your money into a savings bank that pays 5 percent rather than 4 percent. Why? Because, by getting a greater return on your money, you will be getting your money back faster and, therefore, get into profits quicker. The situation gets more complicated and speculative when you have to decide which straight bond to invest in. Of two companies, the lower quality company will sometimes pay the higher return. If economic conditions are good, you would buy the bond paying the highest return because you would be getting your principal back faster. To make an even more complex and speculative decision, you would buy common stock that pays the highest dividend, provided you thought that the dividend was secure. In this way, you would get your original capital back the quickest and start

Companies With Financial Muscle

collecting your profits faster.

WHY GROWTH STOCKS SHOULD BE BOUGHT

But we run into what seems to be quite a paradox when we buy a growth stock, for growth stocks are notoriously stingy dividend payers. The way out of this difficulty is that as the years unfold, the growth company splits its stock and gradually increases its dividends so that you come out actually with a greater return.

Let's take an example. General Motors made its all time high in 1965, so we'll go back ten years to 1956. $1,000 invested at the beginning of 1956 at about $42 a share would give you just about 23 shares. Since there were no stock splits or stock dividends by the end of 1965, you would still have 23 shares. The total dividends received were $674. Looked at another way, you got back over 67 percent on your original capital, or about 6.7 percent in each of the ten years. Since GM made its all time high in 1965, let's assume you sold out half-way between the low and the high at $102. Your 23 shares would now be worth $2,346 and your capital gain would be $1,346 ($2,346 less your original $1,000). This would give you a gain of 135 percent, or 13-1/2 percent average for each of the ten years. Adding the dividends and the capital gain together, you'd come out with $3,020. Again subtracting your original $1,000, your total gain would be $2,020, a little over a 200 percent gain for the ten years, or 20 percent on average per year.

Now let's compare GM with a known growth stock like

Companies With Financial Muscle

IBM. IBM did not top out in 1965 like GM, but went on to more than double, so the figures are very definitely skewed in favor of GM. $1,000 invested at the beginning of 1956 at about $25 per share would give you 40 shares. Over the next ten years, there were five stock splits and two stock dividends, allowing you to come out with 295 shares. After adding up the yearly dividends due to these splits and stock dividends, you would have gotten back $1,823, or 182 percent on your capital, or 18.2 percent per year. That's over 2-1/2 times better than the GM dividend pay-out.

In 1965, the year GM made its all time high, IBM sold between $131 and $178. Let's take the mid-point $154 for our selling price. Your 295 shares would have been worth $45,430 and your capital gain would be $44,430 ($45,430 minus $1,000). This would give you a gain of approximately 4500% average for each of the ten years. This is 33 times better each year than the GM capital gain. Totaling the dividends and the capital gains together, you'd end up with $47,253. Subtracting your original $1,000, your total gain would be $46,253 or 4,625% over the ten years or 462-1/2% on average for each of the ten years.

There is no question that IBM gave you back your money much, much faster and, therefore, built up your profits quicker. That's what investing is all about. Which stock will give you back your initial investment the quickest? I know that IBM is hind-sight, but investors bought and held IBM on some basis. That is what I propose to do—develop some rational ways of selecting a new IBM.

Companies With Financial Muscle

WHAT A GROWTH STOCK IS

What is a growth stock? Be careful, this is not so easy to answer. It is not one in a growing industry. Although we use more electric energy every year, I know of no growth stock in that industry. On the other hand, I do know of growth stocks in cyclical industries. Those are industries which rise and fall with the general economy, like food stores, department stores, and tobacco companies.

A growth company for current purchase is not a *former* growth company either. There are numerous companies that have stopped growing or have much slower rates of growth. I'm thinking of DuPont, Litton Industries, Ling Temco and Memorex.

This brings up the nitty-gritty. Just what is a growth company? *It is an aggressive, creative, well managed company whose earnings in the past few years have been trending upwards and whose present earnings are increasing.* The company can be in any area, from steel making to mobile home manufacturing. Its stock can be traded on the Big Board (the NYSE), the Little Board (the AMEX), or O-T-C (over-the-counter).

Where do we start our detective work? Since the largest number of stocks are traded over-the-counter, we shouldn't be surprised to find most growth companies listed there. But this area has difficulties for the beginner. Published data is harder to come by and research takes more time than the majority of investors have.

The AMEX also has its share of growth companies. But many of them have not been as seasoned as those on

Companies With Financial Muscle

the NYSE, and therefore, financial institutions like banks, mutual funds and pension funds tend to shy away—then so shall we.

That leaves us the NYSE. There are enough growth stocks there that are well seasoned. As such they are even safer investments for the beginner. Here is where we shall look for our pot of gold at the end of the rainbow of stocks.

MY DEFINITION OF A GROWTH STOCK

The earnings rules are very easy to use and locate. Here they are:

1. At the time of the turn-up of the leading indicators, the earnings must have been up for the last 4 years.
2. The corresponding quarters for the last four quarters of the previous 12 months must be up. (If you don't understand this rule, don't worry about it. It'll clear up soon).

WHERE TO FIND GROWTH STOCKS

Where do you start? You need a source for the history of the previous 4 years and the latest 4 quarters in order to establish a trend. The easiest and most available source is the Standard and Poor's Reports. These are called, for those familiar with them, "tear sheets," because they are easily torn out of the ringed notebooks by brokers who mail them to clients. A good public library maintains a set that is updated constantly. If a library is not available, you

Companies With Financial Muscle

can use those at a brokerage house.

HOW TO USE THE STANDARD AND POOR'S STOCK REPORTS

Here is a copy (Figures 2a & 2b) of the front and back of the tear sheet of a stock traded on the NYSE, Houston Natural Gas.

Most of the information can be forgotten. We don't care what the price chart looks like. (We'll get into the movements of stock prices later by using an easier, but more refined method). Nor do we care what the company does for a living. It can manufacture widgits for all we care. Our first concern is with the trend in yearly and quarterly earnings—the financial muscle of the company.

Make yourselves comfortable; be sure you have pencil and paper, glasses, chewing gum, and tissues. Your work is cut out for you. A good idea is to have a partner. Believe me, those few hours of work will be the most rewarding you've ever done.

At the time our leading indicators told us that the market would turn up, one company that met the 4 years earnings increase rule was Houston Natural Gas Corp. Here's the 4 year earnings trend as taken from the back of the tear sheet:

1970=.55, 1971=.58, 1972=.67, 1973=.84, 1974=1.25

Houston must have been doing something right! For each of the above years, no matter what stage the economy was in, this company kept ringing the cash register.

So as to make doubly sure that the current earnings are

HNG[1]   **Houston Natural Gas**   1163

Stock—	Price Mar. 18'77	*P-E Ratio	Dividend	Yield
COMMON............................	33	11	[2]$0.70	[2]2.1%

SUMMARY: Activities of this rapidly growing diversified concern include natural gas transmission, oil and gas exploration and production, the manufacture of industrial gases and coal mining. Rapid development of the coal mining business and expected good increases in oil and gas production enhance the longer-term outlook.

PROSPECTS

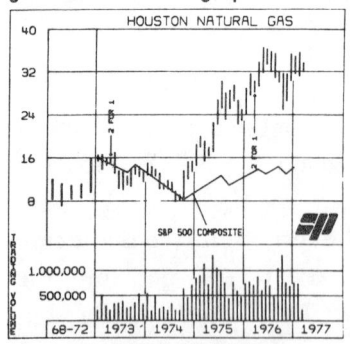

Near Term—Revenues for the fiscal year to end July 31, 1977 should easily exceed the $1.1 billion of the prior year. Gas transmission receipts should advance significantly, due to expected higher volumes (partly reflecting emergency gas sales to supply short interstate pipelines) and higher selling prices. Expanding markets for industrial gases should permit additional good growth from Liquid Carbonic. Despite expected flat shipment levels, moderate revenue growth is anticipated from the coal operation. Oil and gas production receipts should be higher on the strength of probable increases in both volume sales and higher selling prices. Acquisition of Pott Industries would add marine transportation business.

Improved profit contributions are expected from each of the major businesses. Thus, excluding the positive impact on earnings that would result from the acquisition of Pott, share earnings for fiscal 1977 should approximate $3.35, up from the $2.74 reported for the prior year. Dividends should continue at a minimum of $0.17½ quarterly.

Long Term—Good earnings progress is expected, aided by anticipated growing profit contributions from coal and gas production.

REVENUES (Million $)

Period:	1976-7	1975-6	1974-5	1973-4
3Mos.Oct.	287	252	182	92
6Mos.Jan.	696	559	380	204
9Mos.Apr.		850	596	332
12Mos.July		1,121	820	492

Revenues for the six months ended January 31, 1977 advanced 24.5% from those of the corresponding prior-year period. The improvement reflected higher volume throughput and the pass-through of higher gas costs in the transmission business, higher prices and moderate production increases for HNG Oil, and continued good growth in demand for the products of Liquid Carbonic. Volume was restricted by labor strikes in the coal mining operation and production losses at HNG Oil and Zeigler Coal caused by the unusually cold weather early in 1977. While the profit contribution of the coal mining operation was essentially unchanged, each of the three other major businesses were able to achieve good earnings progress. Net income advanced 24.0%. Share earnings rose to $1.68, from $1.36.

RECENT DEVELOPMENTS

HNG acquired in June, 1976, Empire Energy Corp., a Colorado coal mining concern with reserves of about 200 million tons. Total price was $27,500,000.

In March, 1977, HNG agreed in principle to acquire Pott Industries Inc., a diversified energy-related company, for approximately 5,024,000 common shares. The new acquisition of Pott, which earned $20,034,000 in 1976 on revenues of $161,560,000, is subject to a number of conditions and approvals.

DIVIDEND DATA
Payments in the past 12 months were:

[3]**COMMON SHARE EARNINGS ($)**

Period:	1976-7	1975-6	1974-5	1973-4
3Mos.Oct.	0.66	0.57	0.45	0.14
6Mos.Jan.	1.68	1.36	0.96	0.44
9Mos.Apr.		2.08	1.45	0.79
12Mos.July		2.74	2.01	1.25

Amt. of Divd. $	Date Decl.	Ex-divd. Date	Stock of Record	Payment Date
0.15...	Jun. 4	Jun. 8	Jun. 14.	Jul. 1'76
0.15...	Sep. 10	Sep. 14	Sep. 20	Oct. 1'76
0.17½.	Dec. 10	Dec. 14	Dec. 20	Jan. 1'77
0.17½.	Mar. 4	Mar. 8	Mar. 14	Apr. 1'77

[1]Listed N.Y.S.E.; also listed Pacific S.E. options; adj. for 2-for-1 split in Apr. 1976.   [2]Indicated rate.   [3]Assumes conv. of former series A pref. stk. & exercise of certain *Based on latest 12 mos. earns.

STANDARD N.Y.S.E. STOCK REPORTS   **STANDARD & POOR'S CORP.**
© Copyright 1977 Standard & Poor's Corp. Reproduction in whole or in part prohibited except by permission.
Published at Ephrata, Pa. Editorial & Executive Offices, 345 Hudson St., New York, N.Y. 10014

Vol. 44, No. 58   Thursday, March 24, 1977   Sec. 13

FIGURE 2a: Houston Natural Gas (Sample Tear Sheet Side 1)

1163 HOUSTON NATURAL GAS CORPORATION

[1]INCOME STATISTICS (Million $) AND PER SHARE ($) DATA

Year Ended July 31	Total Revs.	%Oper. Inc. of Revs.	Oper. Inc.	Depr., Depl. & Amort.	Net bef. Taxes	Net Inc.	—[2]Common Share ($) Data— Earns.	Divs. Paid	[3]Price Range	Price-Earns. Ratios HI LO
1977--	------	---	-----	----	-----	----	---	0.50	35¾-31¼	----
1976--	1,120.76	17.2	192.54	39.47	148.90	94.76	[4]2.74	0.55	36⅝-24⅜	13- 9
1975--	819.75	18.8	154.35	39.23	104.30	69.65	[4]2.01	0.42½	30¼-14½	15- 7
1974--	491.53	19.4	95.56	28.38	57.93	43.18	[4]1.25	0.26¼	15⅜- 7⅞	12- 6
1973--	316.32	19.0	60.25	21.45	32.01	26.05	[4]0.84	0.17	17 -10⅛	20-12
1972--	277.18	19.5	54.18	17.62	27.53	20.70	[4]0.67	0.16¾	16 - 9⅝	24-14
1971--	243.81	21.7	53.00	17.43	27.77	17.47	[4]0.58	0.16	11⅛- 8⅝	19-15
1970--	201.21	23.7	47.73	15.50	26.46	16.22	[4]0.55	0.16	10⅞- 8½	20-15
1969--	148.52	26.2	38.96	12.19	22.10	13.44	[4]0.48	0.16	11¼- 7¼	23-15
1968--	102.31	29.6	30.33	9.23	15.49	10.85	0.41	0.16	12 - 8⅜	29-20
1967--	86.21	29.6	25.52	8.11	13.37	10.21	0.39	0.14½	11 - 8	28-21

[1]PERTINENT BALANCE SHEET STATISTICS (Million $)

July 31	Gross Prop.	Capital Expend.	Cash Items	Inventories	Receivables	——Current—— Assets	Liabs.	Net Workg. Cap.	Cur. Ratio	Long Term Debt	Share-hldrs. Equity	[2]($) Book Val. Com. Sh.
1976--	741.15	110.85	12.95	49.11	147.34	232.34	198.09	34.25	1.2-1	240.65	372.32	10.24
1975--	711.26	105.50	15.37	50.89	129.15	212.25	168.58	43.67	1.3-1	254.47	296.95	7.94
1974--	612.77	81.50	7.36	30.86	106.98	160.29	118.74	41.56	1.3-1	228.05	244.97	5.82
1973--	527.22	59.43	6.61	19.44	53.81	88.09	72.90	15.19	1.2-1	224.94	188.36	4.55
1972--	473.91	46.69	4.81	18.82	46.81	76.26	62.57	13.68	1.2-1	203.72	167.92	3.88
1971--	524.10	52.79	9.48	15.47	42.37	73.41	60.95	12.46	1.2-1	210.66	144.61	3.16
1970--	483.85	67.23	10.18	12.99	35.76	65.83	60.35	5.47	1.1-1	195.43	133.82	2.75
1969--	392.67	26.36	6.62	11.62	30.07	49.88	41.52	8.36	1.2-1	150.89	122.39	2.29
1968--	263.50	26.69	8.19	4.46	12.39	25.91	28.00	d2.09	0.9-1	107.32	79.70	2.56
1967--	241.27	41.74	11.32	3.23	13.79	29.61	26.09	3.52	1.1-1	107.57	73.12	2.31

[1]Data for 1973 & thereafter as originally reported; data for each yr.prior to 1973 as taken from subsequent yr.'s Annual Report; incl. Zeigler Coal Co., aft. 1973. [2]Adj. for splits of 2-for-1 in April 1976 & April 1973 & 5-for-4 in July 1971 & Jan. 1967. [3]Cal. yr. [4]Based on common shs. & com. sh. equivalents (former series A pref. stk. & certain options). d Deficit.

Fundamental Position

Houston Natural Gas operates transmission facilities for the sale of natural gas to industrial and large commercial customers in the Gulf Coast area of Texas; gas is also sold to utilities and other companies for resale. (HNG's retail gas distribution business was sold to Entex, Inc., in March, 1976.) Major subsidiary activities include coal mining, oil and gas exploration and production, and the production and marketing of industrial gases.

Of fiscal 1976 revenues and income before interest expense and income tax, natural gas and related petrochemical business accounted for 77% and 56%, respectively, industrial gas 14% and 12%, coal 7% and 10%, oil and gas exploration and production 6% and 22%, and intercompany transactions (4%) and nil. Industrial customers accounted for 86% of natural gas revenues, while utility sales accounted for 14%. Average daily delivery of gas was 1.58 billion cf. in fiscal 1976, down from 1.66 billion cf. a year before. Total reserves available on January 1, 1976, under purchase contracts owned through September 1976 were 4.3 trillion cf. Flow through provisions in contracts protect against rapid gas cost increases.

Liquid Carbonic, a wholly owned subsidiary acquired in 1969, supplies carbon dioxide and other compressed gases.

Zeigler Coal, acquired in December, 1973, operates coal mines in Illinois and Kentucky, with 1 billion tons estimated reserves. Production in 1975-6 amounted to 4.6 million tons, up from the 4.2 million tons of the prior year. Production capacity should increase to 11 million tons annually by 1980.

HNG Oil owned at July 31, 1976, 324 net producing gas wells and 121 net oil wells and had 1,090,000 net acres under lease, largely in West Texas. Estimated proved reserves of HNG Oil and HNG Fossil Fuels at the close of 1975-6 were 415.4 billion cf. of gas, 3.4 million bbls. of oil and 1.4 million bbls. of liquid plant products and condensate.

Paid since 1940, dividends averaged 21% of available earnings in the five years through fiscal 1976.

Employees: 7,270. Shareholders: 16,010.

Finances

Capital outlays for fiscal 1977 are projected at $130 million, up from the $111 million of the prior year. HNG placed privately $26 million and $20 million in long-term notes in June, 1973, and October, 1974, respectively, and sold publicly $50 million debentures in January, 1975. In September, 1975, Oasis Pipe Line Co., 50% owned by HNG, privately placed $10 million of first mortgage bonds. In early December, 1976, HNG sold $60 million of debentures.

CAPITALIZATION

LONG TERM DEBT: $300,649,000.
MINORITY INTEREST: $2,392,000.
$4.65 CUM. PREFERRED STOCK: 119,651 shs. ($100 par); privately held.
COMMON STOCK: 34,222,397 shs. ($1 par).

Incorporated in Texas in 1940. **Office**—P. O. Box 1188, Houston, Texas 77001. **Tel**—(713) 654-6161. **Pres**—J. H. Foy. **VP-Secy**—C. Campbell. **VP-Treas**—M. J. Pieri. **Dirs**—R. R. Herring (Chrmn & Chief Exec Officer), C. T. Clagett, J. H. Duncan, J. A. Edwards, W. S. Farish III, O. J. Fleig, J. H. Foy, P. R. Haas, J. M. Harbert, III, R. M. Jenney, R. L. Knauss, M. D. Matthews, N. D. Naiden, C. Rathgeb. **Transfer Agents**—Chase Manhattan Bank, NYC; Texas Commerce Bank, Houston. **Registrars**—Citibank, NYC; First City National Bank, Houston.

Information has been obtained from sources believed to be reliable, but its accuracy and completeness, and that of the opinions based thereon, are not guaranteed. Printed in U. S. A.

FIGURE 2b: Houston Natural Gas [Sample Tear Sheet Side 2]

Companies With Financial Muscle

still growing, we now compare quarterly earnings. These should not be "flat," that is, the same as the corresponding quarter. It goes without saying that neither should the earnings be lower. To check the latest quarters, we look on the front side of the tear sheet.

WATCH THOSE QUARTERLY EARNINGS

A word about quarterly earnings is very important. Four times a year, or every three months, the earnings are published. If you buy a decent daily newspaper, you will be able to catch them during the week. If you can't get daily financial news, by all means buy *Barron's*. This is a weekly Dow-Jones publication which has a section devoted to all the new earnings that have ocurred during the previous week. These earnings are easily identified because the publishers stick an arrow right next to them. This is done for both **NYSE** and **AMEX** stocks, but not in their O-T-C section.

When you spot the latest earnings, they may be bunched up into six months, nine months, or yearly, and must be broken down. Keeping a running tab, quarter by quarter, allows you to do a little subtraction to get the latest quarter. Suppose the nine months earnings appear on a company you're following and read like this:

	1970	1969
9 months	$1.25	$ .92

By subtracting the previous six months earnings, you

obtain a true picture of the latest quarter. Sometimes the cumulative earnings mask an actual decrease in the latest quarter and that means *stay away*.

Another caveat that must be followed is that only corresponding earnings are to be compared—not consecutive ones.

The quarterly earnings for Houston Natural Gas were unfolding like this:

	1974-5	1973-4
3 mo. Oct.	.45 (.45)	.14 (.14)
6 mo. Jan.	.96 (.51)*	.44 (.30)*
9 mo. April	1.45 (.49)	.79 (.35)
12 mo. July	2.01 (.56)	1.25 (.46)

* Since each quarter's earnings as given were cumulative, and since this is deceptive, each quarter's earnings are found by subtracting the previous quarterly earnings from the current cumulative ones.

For example: the 6 months Jan. for 1974-5 was 96 cents. Subtracting the first quarter of 45 cents gives us second quarter earnings of 51 cents. Since this is higher than the corresponding quarter of 30 cents for Jan. 1973-4, our quarterly earnings criterion has been satisfied.

Suppose the January 6 months' earnings for 1974-5 were 71 cents. On the surface this appears to be higher than the corresponding 44 cents. But by breaking it down, the actual quarterly earnings were only 26 cents. Comparing this to the same (corresponding) quarter of 1973-4 of 30 cents, you can see that the latest earnings would have been down. So be careful to always compute the actual

Companies With Financial Muscle

quarterly earnings.

IN A NUT SHELL

Let me repeat:
1. Keep your quarterly earnings up to date.
2. Catch the latest earnings as fast as possible: from a good daily newspaper if you can; from the weekly Barron's if that's all that you can get.
3. Immediately break down the cumulative figures into the latest quarterly figures.
4. Compare only corresponding quarters.

Although we've made a very necessary detour through the tear sheet, we must get back to studying earnings. What to do when the earnings turn down and then turn sharply up is our next consideration.

WHEN TO HOP BACK
ON THE GROWTH COMPANY

The question naturally arises, "suppose the earnings do turn down for one or two quarters and then turn up; when do you buy the stock?" You should be on safe ground when the current quarter is at least 50% higher than the corresponding one. After all, it is very difficult for a company to maintain a quarter-by-quarter increase in earnings. Fine growth companies do get off the track temporarily, so we have to have a method of finding out when they right themselves. Let's examine *Artic Enter-*

Companies With Financial Muscle

prises when it was on the AMEX (now on the NYSE) in 1970 and 1971. The five year earnings looked like this:

1965=.01, 1966=.07, 1967=.21, 1968=.62, 1969=1.19

That's some rate of growth to maintain! The corresponding quarters came out this way:

	1969-70	1967-68
First Quarter	.05	.08
Second Quarter	.06	.05
Third Quarter	.49	.42
Fourth Quarter	1.16	.67

That decrease from .08 to .05 said stay away. But that last quarter of $1.16, up from $.67 a gain of 73%, shouted that Artic was back on the earnings track and, if other things (to be explored later) were correct, it should be bought.

Just to make sure you get this method, here's *Delta Corp. of America*. The four year earnings are continuously up:

1966=.16, 1967=.26, 1968=.51, 1969=.59, 1970=.97

Here's the quarters:

	1970	1969
First Quarter	.14	.14
Second Quarter	.18	.23
Third Quarter	.32	.13
Fourth Quarter	.33	.09

Companies With Financial Muscle

The first quarter was flat—stay clear. The 2nd is down—forget it! But the third quarter shows the old financial muscle: .32 up from .13, an increase of 146%. The 4th quarter verifies it with an increase of 266%!

IN A NUTSHELL

Now that you've been through the maze of quarterly earnings, let's see where we stand. With the leading business indicators turning bullish in May of 1975, we began methodically searching for growth companies to buy. Using the Standard & Poor's Stock Reports on the NYSE, we selected only those companies whose yearly earnings were up for every one of the past 4 years and that also had increasing corresponding quarters for the current, as well as for the previous, three quarters.

All of this analysis of earnings comes under the heading of "fundamentals." You will see easily that by evaluating the earnings trend only, you can be your own analyst. At no time is it necessary to do all of the work that a professional stock analyst does. You don't have to figure out the sales growth, the current ratio, the dilution of earnings because of convertible bonds, the dividend pay-out, the equity per share, the book value, the competition—none of the usual balance sheet analyses.

DON'T WORRY ABOUT THE PRICE-EARNINGS RATIO

Neither should you consider the price-earnings ratio.

Companies With Financial Muscle

This overused and overrated statistic is really a combination of two different elements: the earnings (an important "fundamental"), and the price of the stock (an important "technical" aspect).

The price-earnings ratio, or P/E, of a stock is arrived at quite simply by dividing the latest twelve months earnings into the current price of the stock.

Here are some examples of growth companies at the end of May 1975, the time that the leading indicators gave a "buy" signal. They are not listed in alphabetical order, but by rank order from the lowest to the highest P/E ratio.

OLIN CORP.

The latest 12 months earnings were $4.45 and the price was 26-1/2. (Remember that "the latest 12 months earnings" is not the last fiscal year, but the latest quarter plus the previous three quarters).

$$26.5 \div 4.45 = 5.9$$

This division gives us a P/E of about 6. Olin reached a high in 1976 of 45, producing a 70% gain.

BENDIX CORP.

The latest 12 months earnings were $3.57 and the price was 24-5/8. Dividing the earnings into the price gave a

Companies With Financial Muscle

P/E ratio of 6.89, or about 7 when rounded off.
Bendix hit a high of 46-1/2 in 1976 for a gain of 38%.

SUPER VALUE STORES

The latest 12 months earnings were $1.23 and the price was 11-1/4. Dividing the earnings into the price gave a P/E ratio of 9.14 or about 9 rounded off. The stock hit a high of 24 during 1976 for a gain of 113%.

HOUSTON NATURAL GAS

The latest 12 months earnings were $1.77 and the price was 21-1/4. Dividing the earnings into the price gave a P/E of 12. Houston's stock made a high of 36 in 1977 for a gain of 69%.

The above data has been put together in the following table so you can tell at a glance what happened.

Stock	12 Mo. Earnings	Price	P/E Ratio	% Gain
Olin	4.45	26-1/2	6	70%
Bendix	3.57	24-5/8	7	38%
Super Val.	1.23	11-1/4	9	113%
Houston	1.77	21-1/4	12	69%

As you can see there is no rhyme or reason between the P/E ratio and the percent increase in the price of a stock.

CHAPTER 4

THE KEY TO THE VAULT—
Or When To Buy And Sell Each Growth Stock

We have learned how to anticipate the turn-up in the business cycle, and therefore the stock market, by using the leading indicators. We've developed a system of zeroing in on the growth companies we're going to buy by evaluating the 4 year growth record and the latest four quarters. Now we're going to get into timing techniques that will tell us not only when to buy, but also when to sell.

This propels us into an even more esoteric area of the market—the "technical." The technical tools are as varied as the cut pieces of a jigsaw puzzle. The technicians have literally dissected all the ingredients that make up the market movements themselves, so that there is not much else to be done except to select a timing device that is not only easy to use, but which works.

The Key To The Vault

WHAT IS MEANT BY THE TECHNICAL ASPECT OF THE MARKET

The technical aspects of the market are those indicators which come from the market itself. These are broken down into two broad areas: Volume and Price Movement. The technicians say that everything that is known by anybody, both public and private information, must eventually show up in the activities of individuals and groups as they continuously buy and sell. In other words, all knowledge, past, present, and future, about a company must be translated into the amount of buying and selling (volume), and the changes in the stock's price.

There are roughly two schools of thought in the technical area: those who believe only in the changes in prices, and those who deal with volume only. Of course, there are the marriage brokers who have systems using both price and volume.

THE POINT AND FIGURE METHOD

One of the oldest systems to use only price movements is the "point and figure" method. These technicians claim that the changes in prices affect the volume. When it is seen that there are large price changes, more and more traders tend to jump on the bandwagon, thus creating more than usual volume.

The "point and figure" method considers only price changes, not time or volume. The price changes also have to be in definite amounts, much the same as the discrete

The Key To The Vault

number of electrons in an atom. The usual price change is $1.00, although some use $.50 for stocks under $10 a share and $2.00 a unit for stocks over $100 a share. All fractions are ignored. The system depends on two elements: the current trend of the price movement and the reversal of that trend. If a reversal is defined as having the first price trend turn in the opposite direction by at least three minimum units, then we have the heart of the modern 3 point reversal point and figure charts.

Suppose a stock moved upward from 14-3/4 to 15-1/2, to16-1/4, to 18-3/4, to 20 and to 21-3/8. Here's how you would draw your point and figure chart to make the first price trend. Remember that since $1.00 is the unit, you are to drop all the fractions and round down to the nearest dollar. Your new series will look like this: 15, 16, 17, 18, 19, 20, 21. On the chart paper, it will appear this way:

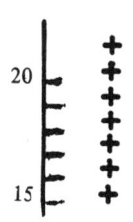

```
       +
   20  +
       +
       +
       +
       +
   15  +
```

The second part of the system is the reversal. Prices have to turn down for at least 3 units before this happens. Suppose the prices back down like this: 20-3/4, 19-1/4, 18, 17-3/4, 17-1/2, 17. Your series will turn out to be: 20, 19, 18, 17. The downward reversal will be triggered by the drop to 18. The point and figure chart will now look like

The Key To The Vault

this:

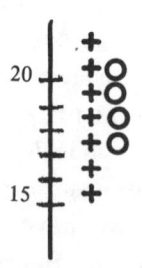

```
      |  +
   20 +  +O
      |  +O
      |  +O
      |  +O
      |  +
   15 +  +
      |
```

You now have one up column and one down column. Since this price movement could have taken two months, you can usually get one year's price changes on a small chart. Time does not appear on this kind of chart.

The question now comes up, so what? What do you do with these chicken scratches? Bear with me one moment, please. Suppose, in our example, prices reverse upwards: 17-1/2, 18-1/4, 18-3/4, 20-1/4, 21, 22-1/4. This series will show up as 17, 18, 19, 20, 21, 22. The reversal upwards makes our third column.

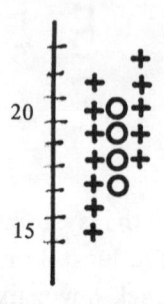

```
      |      +
      |   + +
   20 |  +O+
      |  +O+
      |  +O+
      |  +O
      |  +
   15 +  +
      |
```

That price of 22 is *very important*. It means that a break-out has occurred, making the stock *bullish*. The fact that the latest reversal upward trend could clear the

50

The Key To The Vault

barrier at 21 shows that there is more bullish than bearish pressure. This is where many of the point and figure chartists buy.

How do they know where to sell out their long position? There are several methods, depending upon congestion areas (places where the price oscillates up and down indecisively) and on the horizontal or vertical "counts" taken in those areas. There are also trend lines and channels that may be used. The simplest way is to let a down reversal column slip below the previous down column. Like this:

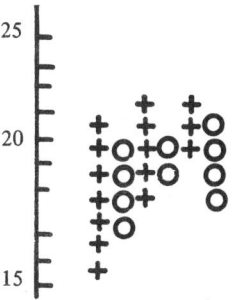

```
25 ┤
   ┤          +  +
   ┤        + + +O
20 ┤       +O+O+O
   ┤       +O+O O
   ┤       +O+  O
   ┤       +O   O
15 ┤       +
```

That last column down to 18 got below the previous down column which had stopped at 19. That's where the point and figurer gets stopped out.

These are the highlights of this system and since it is too demanding for the average person, we will *not* use it. In passing, I do think it is a good one to use.

THE DAILY BAR CHART

Another system that depends on price movement alone

The Key To The Vault

is the daily bar chart. Here, time is an integral feature. The daily range of a stock is drawn with a vertical line and a little horizontal notch is hooked onto it showing the close. Every day the stock trades are plotted. Suppose you read in the paper the following:

		High	Low	Close	Net Change
Monday	6-1	16-7/8	15-3/4	16-1/4	1/4
Tuesday	6-2	17-1/2	16-1/8	17-1/4	1
Wed.	6-3	18-3/8	16-7/8	18-3/8	1-1/8
Thurs	6-4	18-1/8	17-1/2	17-3/4	5/8
Fri.	6-5	19-3/4	17-3/8	19-1/2	1-3/4

Ignore the net change, and plot the rest like the following:

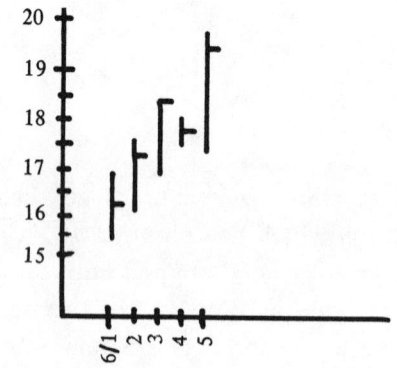

The ranges are vertical strokes, the closes are horizontal notches, and time is measured along the horizontal axis.

MOVING AVERAGES

Once these prices have been plotted, several systems

The Key To The Vault

can be applied to this data. The most practiced is the "moving" average. A moving average is just what you learned in the seventh grade. You take so many days, add up the closes, and divide by the number of days. A ten day moving average would mean the addition of the closes for the last ten days and then dividing this sum by ten. On the eleventh day, you add this to the preceding nine days (don't forget to drop the first day) and divide by ten again. As time goes on, you will get a rather smooth trend of the closing prices.

That's what you want—a smooth curve that eliminates a great deal of the erraticness of the daily price fluctuations. This curve is usually made by moving averages of 150 and 50 trading days, the former given the misnomer of the 200 day moving average and the latter, the ten week moving average.

The moving average system is easy to use. Keep in mind that the M-A will be overhead (above the current price) if the stock is bearish. As current prices stabilize, the M-A will gradually stop its downward bias and go horizontal, generally staying above the prices. At some point, if the prices start up, the M-A line will be penetrated. It is at this juncture—as the prices twirl up through the M-A—that the chartist would buy and hold on until the reverse penetration occurs. As prices rise, the M-A line would bend upwards and stay under the prices. As a top was made, the M-A would flatten out and the sell signal would occur when the prices broke below the M-A line.

Needless to say that the longer the *time* used for the M-A, the longer it will take for both the buy and sell

The Key To The Vault

signals to occur. This means that you won't be getting in or out as fast as you might want, which could cost more "points" than necessary.

To prevent this, a M-A of shorter duration, such as the 10 week average, may be used. However, this can sometimes lead to other difficulties—the "whip-saw." On some occasions, prices may burst up through the 10 week M-A only to nose down again forcing you to sell out only a short time after you bought.

It is frankly admitted that there isn't any method, technical or fundamental, that doesn't have its share of these needless "whip-saw" losses. Once again, like the point and figure method, this is a good system, but is too time-consuming for most people. Of course, you can subscribe to a good chart service that puts these M-A's on the price charts. But don't worry about it—we'll be developing our own simple, yet workable, technical system.

Another group that uses only price movements is the "cycle" bunch. These technicians believe that all stocks move in cycles, many of which are predictable. They count the weeks, or days, between a particular stock's lows. If the pattern is 3-1/2 weeks, then they buy at those cyclical lows and sell out near the cyclical highs. One of the difficulties is that sometimes you get cycles within cycles and the interpretation becomes sticky.

THE ELLIOTT WAVE THEORY

Then there are those who use the "Elliott Wave"

theory. Elliott held that all stock price trends, whether minor movements or major cycles, are made up of a fixed number of "waves" or fluctuations. These waves occur in a definite order or rhythm, but do not have the same extent or duration. Elliott contended that these "waves" represent a natural law which controls price movements.

According to Elliott, bull markets are composed of five primary waves, three of which are upward and two downward. The upward waves are always composed of five intermediate waves. Each of the three intermediate advancing waves is composed of five minor waves. Bear markets and all other corrections between advancing waves are made up of three waves.

For example, if we give numbers in sequence to the five waves composing an uptrend, 1, 3, and 5 are up, and each is made up of five smaller waves. The downward corrections 2 and 4, however, are composed of three waves instead of five.

Figure 3a shows the whole bull market move.

1. The five primary waves are: "0" to "1", "1" to "2", "2" to "3", "3" to "4", and "4" to "5".

2. The three upward waves are: "0" to "1", "2" to "3", and "4" to "5".

3. The two downward waves are "1" to "2", and "3" to "4".

4. Each of the advancing waves is composed of five minor waves. For example, the first upward wave, "0" to "1", has the five minor waves: "0" to (1), (1) to (2), (2) to (3), (3) to (4), and (4) to (5).

5. Each of the down waves have been redrawn in Figures 3b and 3c in order to avoid confusion. The down

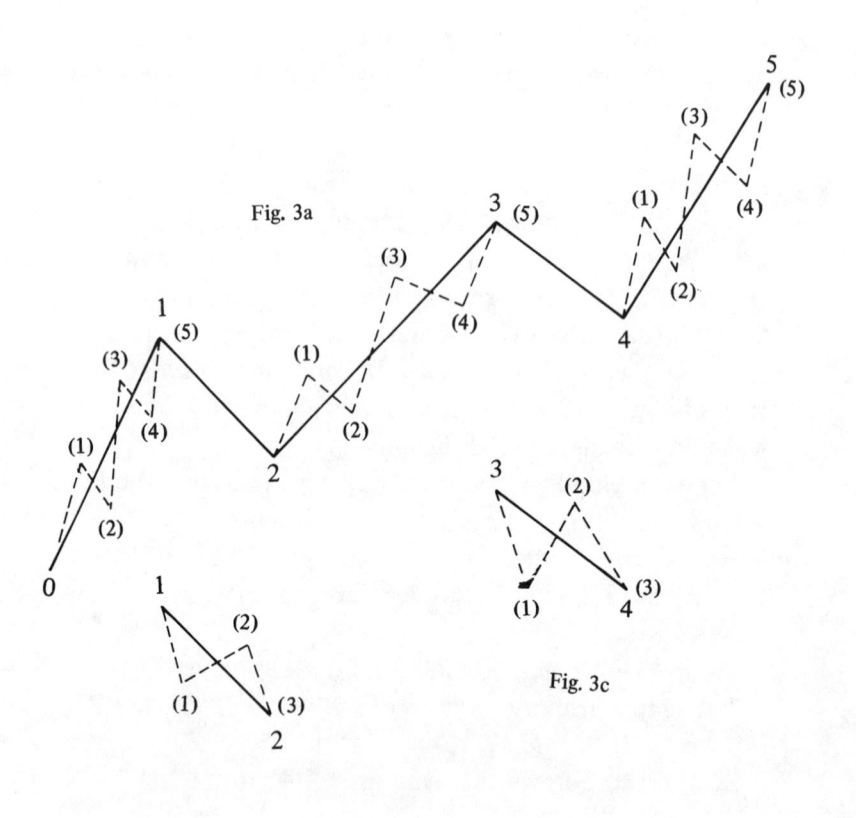

**FIGURE 3a, b, c:
Elliott Bull Market [b and c Represent Downwaves]**

wave "1" to "2" is made up of the three minor waves: "1" to (1), (1) to (2), and (2) to (3).

The difficulty with this method lies in the confusion that comes about from trying to identify the correct waves as they develop. Sometimes there are even extensions of waves which can only be seen with hindsight. This technique is too difficult for most market players.

THE RELATIVE STRENGTH CONCEPT

Another large group of technicians specializing in price movements are those that utilize "relative strength." They try to figure out which stocks act stronger or weaker than the market. If the market advanced 1% for the week and a stock increased 2%, then the stock was twice as strong as the market. If the market went up 1% and the stock also legged up 1%, the stock was neutral. If the market perked up 1% and the stock decreased 1%, the stock was twice as weak. To keep track of a lot of stocks, a computer is needed. With a few stocks you can do it on your own with some arithmetic and chart paper. Fortunately, the method that we will use gives comparable results and is far less time consuming.

DON WORDEN'S TICK VOLUME

There is a group of technicians who use volume as the key to stock success. Don Worden is one of the pioneers of a system called "tick" volume. The idea behind this was

The Key To The Vault

simple, but the application was enervating before the advent of the computer.

Don assumes that if a stock trades at a higher price, this must be accumulation. If a trade occurs at the lower price, this is distribution. Trades at the same price—"even ticks"—are to be neglected since they don't materially affect the results.

After the close, computer tapes of all the transactions on both the NYSE and AMEX are computer sorted. All volume made on "upticks" is added together for one total. All the volume occurring on "downticks" is added for another total. These two totals are then added algebraically for the final day's net results. As this is done day after day and week after week, he has a quantitative measure to determine whether the stock is under accumulation or distribution.

Although, on the surface, "tick volume" seems to be the final answer, in practice, it has not proven so. For one thing, the rules prohibiting short sales on downticks make it impossible to distinguish between buying and selling. To a computer, programmed to assign all volume at higher transactions to the accumulation side of the equation, short sales can be very misleading.

A second limitation is that not all the volume is shown on the exchange's tapes. Large block transactions now take place in the "third market" and on the "q.t." Nobody can find out the true volume figures. At best, "tick volume" is only helpful. We certainly will not be using it.

Then there are those technicians who combine volume and price. Don Worden is one. He has combined his "tick volume" with point and figure charts. Perhaps the leading

The Key To The Vault

technicians of combining the daily bar chart and volume are Edwards and Magee. They wrote the "bible" called, *"Technical Analysis of Stock Trends."*

THE CONFIGURATIONS OF EDWARDS & MAGEE

Edwards and Magee look for reversal patterns on their bar charts that are confirmed by volume. Using their methods is like playing the market with Euclid. They analyze head-and-shoulders, saucers, triangles, rectangles, diamonds, wedges, flags, pennants, gaps, basic trendlines and channels. The study of these geometrical patterns is fascinating, educating, useful, and very time-consuming. They are for market buffs who want to dazzle their friends. But, they are not for us—too complicated and subject to biased interpretation.

MY OWN WEEKLY MINOR TREND RULES

We will use what I call the "weekly minor trend" rule. It is simple to plot—the information comes from the Saturday or Sunday newspaper, or the weekly Barron's, and is not subject to any individual interpretation.

A minor trend is applicable to anything that fluctuates over any period of time. All oscillating entities have surges and retreats, peaks and valleys, ups and downs. In fact, whole philosophies have been built on this phenomenon. Hegel's dialectic of "thesis, antithesis, and synthesis" comes to mind. Dow Theory is based on this back and

The Key To The Vault

forth movement.

The idea is not only simple and very easy to apply, but quite workable in its success. Suppose I make the price of a stock fluctuate, as in this example:

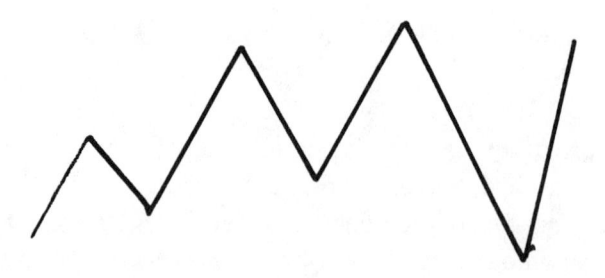

When the peak, #2, thrusts above the peak at #1, the "minor trend" is bullish. After the down-leg, #4, drops below the valley at #3, the "minor trend" is bearish. That's almost all there is to it. Consider the illustration below:

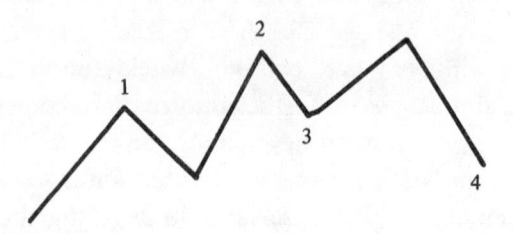

As soon as the peak at #2 got higher than the peak at #1, the "minor trend" rule said the stock was bullish. When #4 fell below #3, the "minor trend" rule said that the stock was bearish.

The Key To The Vault

Sometimes a dip will just nip under a previous valley only to thrust up again.

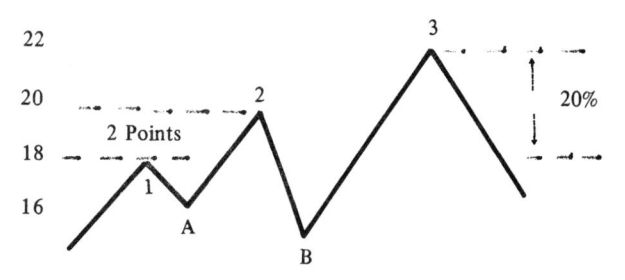

```
22                          3
20            2                    20%
         2 Points
18
         1
16
          A
            B
```

The dip at #B, under the previous low at #A, proves to be a whip-saw. No sooner would we have sold out than the price jumps upward and bursts over the peak at #2. To prevent this whip-sawing, we add one qualification to our rule. Each buy signal must have an upward thrust over the preceding peak by at least 2 points (dollars). Each sell signal must have a downward thrust from the highest closing price of at least 20%.

Here is my "weekly minor trend" rule in a nutshell:

1. Only the weekly closes are plotted. (Volume plays no part in this technique). The weekly close is actually Friday's close. It can easily be found in the Saturday or Sunday paper, or in Barron's.

2. A "buy" signal occurs when prices go up, then down, and then go up again, this time getting above the preceding peak by at least 2 points. (This two points applies to all price levels over $10. Under $10 use one point).

3. A sell signal occurs when prices thrust down below the highest close by at least 20%. (Do *not* use this sell

61

The Key To The Vault

signal if you can't at least get your round trip commissions back. Of course, if the latest quarterly earnings just turned flat (the same) or were down from last year's corresponding earnings, then sell, even if it means taking a loss).

4. If you sold profitably on the "weekly trend" sell rule signal, you can go long again on the next "weekly minor trend" rule buy signal, as long as the current quarterly earnings are higher and the leading indicators are bullish.

The reasoning behind the caveat in rule 3 should be clear. You can analyze the balance sheet until you are blue in the face. You can private-eye competition, insider transactions, the president and the executive board, and the companies assets and liabilities. When you get down to the mat, however, the most important element is earnings. As long as they are increasing and as long as the leading indicators are up, you are in good shape.

In any bull market, there are always reactions, some of which are severe enough to turn the whole market, including your holdings, into bear moves. No matter what technical system you use—point and figure charts, relative strength, bar charts or my "weekly minor trend" rule—you will get reversals from bullish to bearish moves.

These turn-downs will produce "whip-saws." That is, you will be taking a series of losses that you shouldn't be. In the examples that follow, you'll see the wisdom of the caveats of rule 3.

Earnings were spoken of extensively in the preceding material. I cannot over-emphasize the primary reliance on earnings over the use of the purely technical signals. Everyone who deals with the market should hang a neon

The Key To The Vault

sign up in his work room that keeps flashing, Earnings!, Earnings!, Earnings!

As soon as the earnings on any of these growth stocks turn flat or down, it should be sold outright. Sometimes the word gets around before the earnings become public so that you will get a technical sell signal first. Sometimes you get lucky and are able to act quickly enough to save some money before you have to sell at the lower "weekly trend" rule signal.

Conversely, as long as those quarterly earnings are up, there is no reason not to take another long position in a stock if you get a buy on the "weekly trend" rule. You will see this happening in some examples.

It may even happen that you already have one long position, get a sell signal which would give you a "paper" loss, so that you must still hold the stock, then get another buy signal so that you add another position, and wind up making a lot of money on both.

You will find that the results are about the same as you get with the much more complicated relative strength measurements, and you will be able to buy and sell faster than if you use point and figure charts. The four rules are simple and not subject to the frustration of emotional interpretation that leads to "whip-saws," the taking of losses unnecessarily.

ILLUSTRATIONS OF THE MINOR TREND RULE

In the illustrations that follow there is no mention of the kind of businesses the companies are in. As pointed out

The Key To The Vault

earlier, it makes no difference what a company does for its profits. As long as it makes more and more money we will be very happy and successful.

ALLIED STORES

These are the 4 yearly increases in earnings:

1974 =	$4.59	4th yearly increase
1973 =	3.98	3rd yearly increase
1972 =	3.27	2nd yearly increase
1971 =	2.35	1st yearly increase
1970 =	1.71	

(These were taken from the back of the tear sheet).

Barron's reported earnings on March 31, 1975. They were for the twelve months ending January, 1975, and were $4.39 versus $3.63.

Let's see if the earnings were up for that last quarter.

	1975	1974
1st quarter	.52	.45
2nd quarter	.61	.27
3rd quarter	1.17	.50
4th quarter	2.29	1.95
Year's total	4.59	3.17

Allied stores met our two earnings rules:

1. The earnings were up for the last 4 years.

2. Each of the previous 4 corresponding quarters were higher.

Now we can go on with the charting. The prices of each

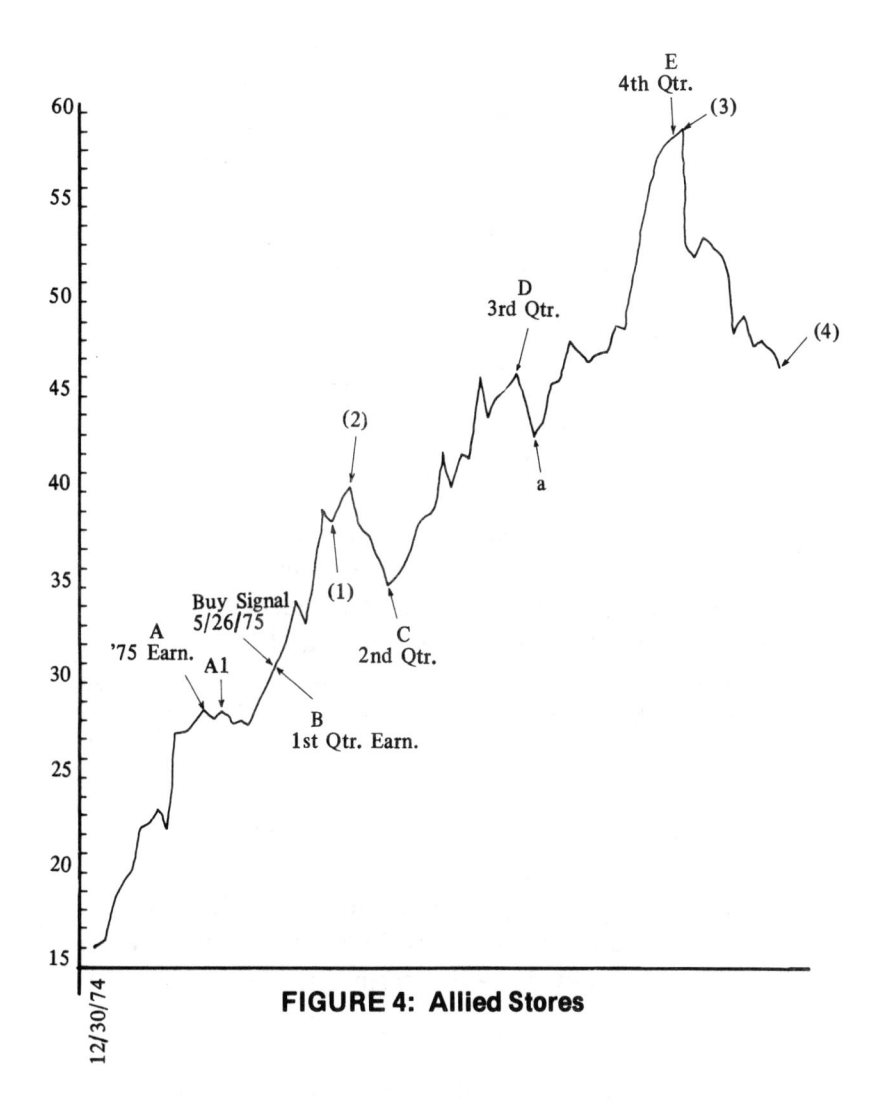

FIGURE 4: Allied Stores

65

The Key To The Vault

week's close are taken from Barron's and are plotted as shown in Figure 4. In this way you will also see the latest earnings reports that Barron's publishes as soon as they come out, because you'll see an arrow pointing to them.

In order to simplify the explanation, I'll use the numbers and letters on the chart to designate the points of interest. As the figures unfolded each week from Barron's, you can see what I did.

Remember that the leading indicators gave a "buy signal" at the end of May, 1975. That was when the stock was bought for 30-3/8.

POINT "A"

The 1975 earnings had come out before the stock was bought. The earnings were broken down on a yearly and quarterly basis as shown above. All I needed to convince myself to buy were two things more, and I got them: the leading indicators had to turn up and a "minor trend breakout" had to occur.

POINT "B"

The break-out is more than 2 points higher than the rally point at "A1." The leading indicators say buy. As a coincidence, the first quarter earnings for 1976 came out. For the first quarter they were 52 cents versus 45 cents; just what we wanted—better earnings.

POINT "C"

From a peak of 40-1/4 prices fell to 35. Since this retracement was 13% and fell short of our 20% rule, we are still long. (I have to admit it was a cliff hanger).

The Key To The Vault

Earnings for the second quarter came out in August, 1975. They were $1.13 versus $.72 for the six months. But what were they for the second quarter alone? Let's see:

2nd quarter	1.13	.72	
1st quarter	.52	.45	(Subtract)
	.61	.27	

They're just what we're looking for—higher earnings.

POINT "D"

Third quarter earnings showed up in Barron's. They were $2.30 versus $1.22. But, were they up for this quarter?

3rd quarter	2.30	1.22	
2nd quarter	1.13	.72	(Subtract)
	1.17	.50	

POINT "E"

Fourth quarter earnings came out: $6.89 versus $4.39 for the year. Were those for the fourth quarter higher?

4th quarter	6.89	4.39	
3rd quarter	2.30	1.22	(Subtract)
	4.59	3.17	

Great Earnings!

POINT "4"

What tough luck! Only one week after such fine earnings, the price tops out at 57-5/8 and goes into a nose

The Key To The Vault

dive. We must sell at 45-1/2 because this exceeded our 20% rule of retracement from the top of the move.

Altogether we grossed 15-1/8 points (45-1/2—30-3/8). The time period we held the stock was from May, 1975 to June, 1976. For just one year's time we made about 50% on our investment. Well worth the trouble, wasn't it?

AMETEK

These are the 4 yearly increases in earnings:

1974=$2.21	4th yearly increase
1973=$1.80	3rd yearly increase
1972=$1.28	2nd yearly increase
1971=$ .92	1st yearly increase
1970=$ .76	

(These were taken from the back of the tear sheet).

Barron's reported earnings on February 17, 1975. They were for the twelve months ending December, 1974, and were $2.21 versus $1.80.

Let's see if the earnings were up for that last quarter.

	1974	1973
1st quarter	.50	.39
2nd quarter	.62	.46
3rd quarter	.55	.49
4th quarter	.54	.46
	2.21	1.80

Ametek met our two earnings rules:

The Key To The Vault

1. The earnings were up for each of the last 4 years.
2. Each of the previous 4 corresponding quarters were higher.

Now we can go on with the charting. Once again we use Barron's closing prices and new earnings as shown in Figure 5.

Numbers and letters will be used to designate the places of interest.

POINT "A"

The 1974 earnings had come out before the stock was bought. They were broken down on a yearly and quarterly basis as shown in Figure 5. The first quarterly earnings for 1975 came out on April 21, 1975. They were higher: 60 cents versus 50 cents.

POINT "1"

Ametek was bought at 16-3/4 when the leading indicators gave a "buy" signal. The price of the stock had already risen the necessary 2 points over the last rally, which was at point "A."

POINT "B"

Second quarter earnings came out. Let's see if they were higher for the quarter:

2nd quarter	1.32	1.12	
1st quarter	.60	.50	(Subtract)
	.72	.62	

Just what we hoped, higher earnings.

69

FIGURE 5: Ametek

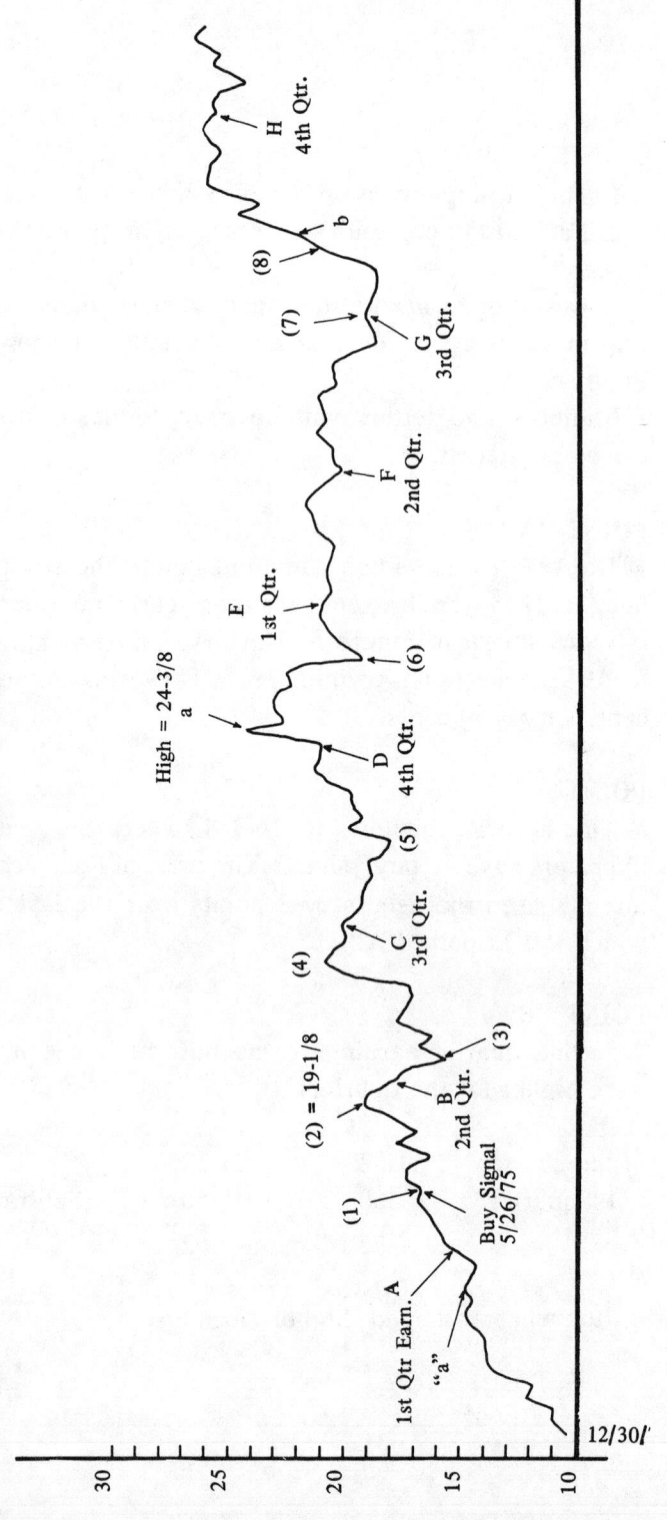

The Key To The Vault

POINT "3"

There was a "shake-out" from the high of 19-1/8 to 15-5/8. This reaction was a little over 18%, not enough for us to sell on our "20% dip rule."

POINT "C"

Third quarter earnings showed up in Barron's. They were for nine months September: $1.94 versus $1.67. Breaking them down:

3rd quarter	1.94	1.67
2nd quarter	1.32	1.12
	.62	.55

Fine, they were higher.

POINT "5"

This shake-out from 20-3/4 to 18-1/8 wasn't enough to trigger a sell. The dip was about 12-1/2%—not the 20% we needed.

POINT "D"

Fourth quarter earnings appeared in Barron's. They were for the twelve months ending December: $2.55 versus $2.21. Were they better for this last quarter?

4th quarter	2.55	2.21
3rd quarter	1.94	1.67
	.61	.54

Yes they were, so stay long.

The Key To The Vault

POINT "6"

This retracement is hairy. From a high of 24-3/8, Ametek slips to 19-7/8 or 18-1/2%. Close to our 20% sell rule, but we're still in there.

POINT "E"

First quarter earnings showed up in Barron's. They were higher: 66 cents versus 60 cents. Stay long.

POINT "F"

Second quarter earnings: six months June were $1.43 versus $1.32. How were they for this quarter?

2nd quarter	1.43	1.32	
1st quarter	.66	.60	(Subtract)
	.77	.72	

They're better, so hang in there.

POINT "G"

Third quarter earnings: nine months September were $2.17 versus $1.94.

3rd quarter	2.17	1.94	
2nd quarter	1.43	1.32	(Subtract)
	.74	.62	

Ametek is still increasing its earnings. Stay with it.

POINT "8"

Fourth quarter earnings appeared in Barron's on

The Key To The Vault

February 7, 1977. They were for twelve months December: $2.84 versus $2.55.

4th quarter	2.84	2.55	
3rd quarter	2.17	1.94	(Subtract)
	.67	.61	

Hold the stock.

At the close of the chart, March 28, 1977, Ametek was 29-3/4. Since the stock was bought for 16-3/4, the gross profit was 13 points, or over 77%—and the stock was still being held for further gains.

BENDIX CORP.

These are the 4 yearly increases in earnings:

1974=$4.65	4th yearly increase
1973= 4.19	3rd yearly increase
1972= 3.56	2nd yearly increase
1971= 2.56	1st yearly increase
1970= 1.95	

(These were taken from the back of the tear sheet. The latest tear sheet will not show these earnings because of a recent 4 for 3 stock split. To get the comparable figures, take the 1970 earnings on the present tear sheet of $1.95 and multiply by 3/4. You would get the $1.46 that shows up on the latest tear sheet for 1977. If you do the same for the rest of the years, you will get a comparable match).

73

The Key To The Vault

A check on the quarterly earnings, as plotted and shown in Figure 6, showed the last four quarters were also higher.

POINT "A"

Now for the latest earnings. Barron's reported earnings on May 5, 1975. They were for six months ending March: $2.21 versus $2.10. Were they higher for the quarter?

2nd quarter	1.15	1.11
1st quarter	1.06	.99
	2.21	2.10

So far, so good. All that was needed was for the leading indicators to give a "buy" signal.

POINT "2"

The leading indicators gave a go-ahead signal here. Immediately afterwards, Bendix gave a leap upward so that point "2" exceeded point "1" by over two points.

The Stock was bought at 38-7/8.

POINT "B"

Nine months earnings appeared in Barron's: $3.54 versus $3.36. Were they better?

3rd quarter	3.54	3.36	
2nd quarter	2.21	2.10	(Subtract)
	1.33	1.26	

FIGURE 6: Bendix

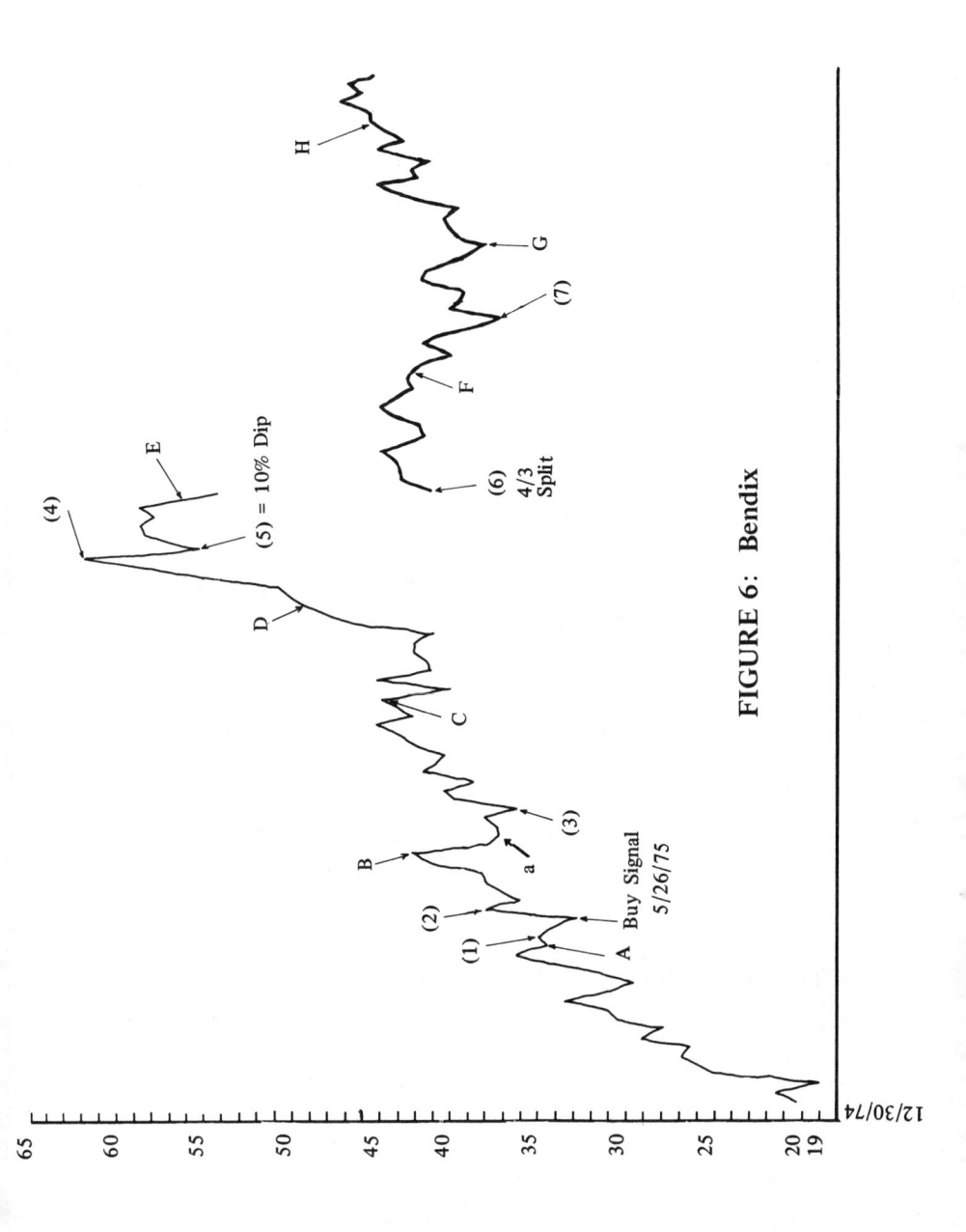

75

The Key To The Vault

Yes they were, so hold on.

POINT "3"

This is a typical shake-out; from 43 down to 37-1/8. Since this was only a 14% retracement, not a 20% one, we're still in.

POINT "C"

Barron's reports twelve months earnings: $4.89 versus $4.65. How good were these?

4th quarter	4.89	4.65	
3rd quarter	3.54	3.36	(Subtract)
	1.35	1.29	

They were O.K.

POINT "D"

Another earnings report: three months December were $1.42 versus $1.05.

Fine.

POINT "5"

Bendix peaked out at 61-3/4 and sold off to 55-1/2. Was this enough to get us out? No, since the dip was only 10%.

POINT "E"

New earnings for six months were for March: $2.26 versus $1.65.

The Key To The Vault

2nd quarter	2.26	1.65
1st quarter	1.42	1.05
	.84	.60

Good, they were better.

POINT "6"

On April 19, 1976, Barron's showed a stock split of four for three. This means that for every three shares you'd be getting one more. If you already owned 300 shares, you'd now have 400. If you originally held 100 shares, you now hold 133-1/3 shares. (The third of a share would be paid off in cash if you didn't want to pay additional money to round it off to one whole share).

I adjusted the new stock price by drawing a new scale approximating the old one. Since the split price in Barron's was 41, I multiplied 41 by 4/3 and got approximately 55 on the old price scale. That is where I started to plot the new split prices.

POINT "F"

New nine months earnings reported: $3.59 versus $2.65.

3rd quarter	3.59	2.65	
2nd quarter	2.26	1.65	(Subtract)
	1.33	1.00	

They're higher so stick with it.

The Key To The Vault

POINT "7"

The shake-out from 37-1/2 from the high was very close to selling us out. If prices had closed at 37 or lower we would have had to sell. Instead, up they went.

POINT "G"

New yearly earnings for twelve months ending in December were $4.74 versus $3.66.

4th quarter	4.74	3.66	
3rd quarter	3.59	2.65	(Subtract)
	1.15	1.01	

They're higher. Sit tight.

POINT "H"

First quarter earnings were $1.10 versus $1.06. Since they're higher we're still long.

What's our over-all profit at this time? The original cost on 100 shares at 38-7/8 was about $4000. What is the investment worth now?: After the split we owned 133 shares. 133 times the price at which our chart stops (which was 45-1/2) equals $6018. This profit of $2018 comes to about 50%.

BORDEN, INC.

These are the 4 yearly increases in earnings:

The Key To The Vault

1974 = $2.72	4th yearly increase
1973 = 2.37	3rd yearly increase
1972 = 2.18	2nd yearly increase
1971 = 2.00	1st yearly increase
1970 = 1.83	

(These were taken from the back of the tear sheet).

Barron's reported earnings on March 17, 1975. They were for twelve months ending December, 1974, and were $2.72 versus $2.37.

Let's see if the earnings were up for that last quarter.

	1974	1973
1st quarter	.58	.51
2nd quarter	.81	.69
3rd quarter	.72	.59
4th quarter	.61	.58
	2.72	2.37

Borden met our two earnings rules:
1. The earnings were up for the last four years.
2. Each of the previous four quarters were higher.

Now we can do the charting as shown in Figure 7.

POINT "A"

The earnings for 1974 came out and were $2.72 versus $2.37. This made the fourth quarter earnings equal to 61 cents as against 58 cents.

POINT "B"

The first quarterly earnings showed up in Barron's.

FIGURE 7: Bordens

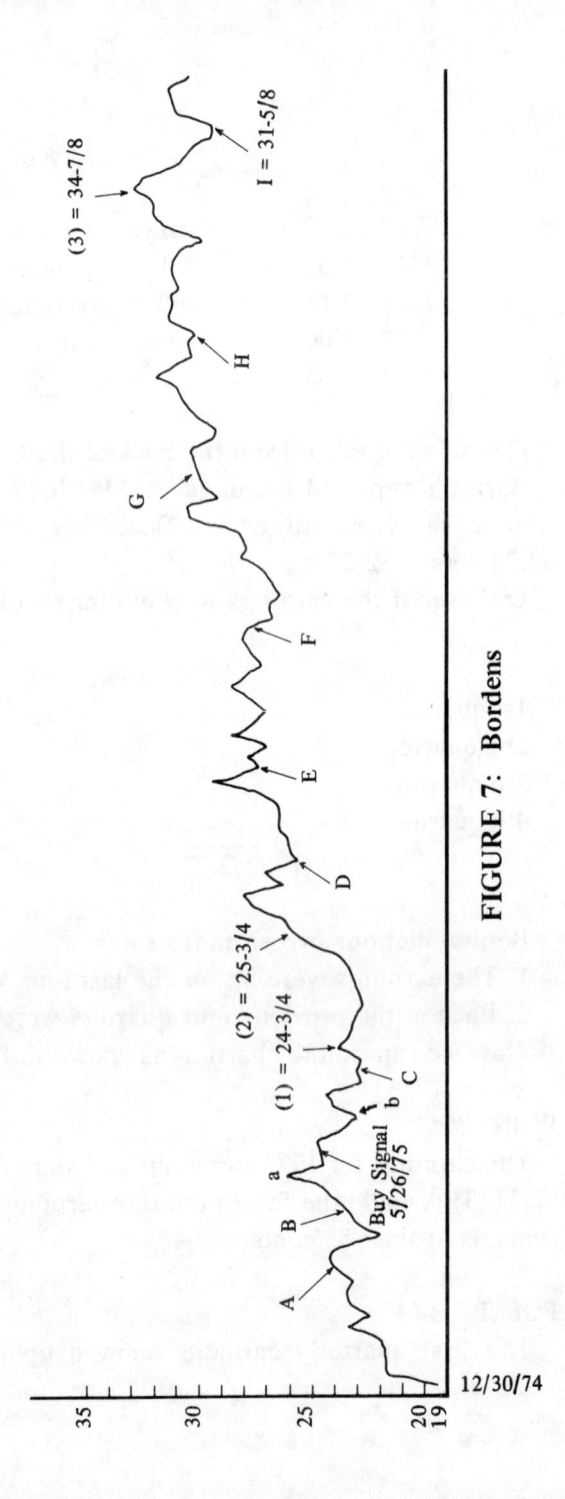

The Key To The Vault

They were, as described above, 61 cents versus 58 cents.

POINT "C"

Six months earnings came out. They were $1.47 versus $1.39. Were they higher for the quarter?

2nd quarter	1.47	1.39	
1st quarter	.61	.58	(Subtract)
	.86	.81	

Yes, they were higher.

It should be noted that although the leading indicators gave a buy signal in May of 1975, this stock did not. Only at point "2", after almost five months went by, was a purchase made.

POINT "2"

Borden finally breaks out at 25-3/4. This meets our two point break-out rule exactly. (The price had to close over the previous bulge of 23-3/4 by at least two points).

POINT "D"

Nine months earnings came in at $2.30 versus $2.11. Here's the break-down:

3rd quarter	2.30	2.11	
2nd quarter	1.47	1.39	(Subtract)
	.83	.72	

POINT "E"

Twelve months earnings were $3.01 versus $2.72. This

The Key To The Vault

is what the last quarter looked like:

4th quarter	3.01	2.72	
3rd quarter	2.30	2.11	(Subtract)
	.71	.61	

Hold the Stock.

POINT "F"

New earnings for the first quarter were 74 cents versus 61 cents. Stay with it.

POINT "G"

Six months earnings:

2nd quarter	1.80	1.47	
1st quarter	.74	.61	(Subtract)
	1.06	.86	

They are higher. Maintain the position.

POINT "H"

Nine months earnings were reported:

3rd quarter	2.79	2.30	
2nd quarter	1.80	1.47	(Subtract)
	.99	.83	

Better earnings. Stay long.

The Key To The Vault

POINT "I"

Twelve months earnings ending December were $3.64 versus $3.01.

4th quarter	3.64	3.01	
3rd quarter	2.79	2.30	(Subtract)
	.85	.71	

Again the earnings were higher. Continue to hold.

Note that the shake-out from 34-7/8 at point "3" to 31-5/8 at point "I" was only a dip of a little over 9%, not even half enough to stop us out.

The chart stops with the price at 32-7/8. Since the stock was bought at 25-3/4, this gave a gross profit of over 27%—and the stock was still being held.

CHAPTER 5

PLAY IT AGAIN, SAM—
Or Let's See If You Can Do It

In order to see if you understand these rules, I'm going to give you the raw data just as it appeared in Barron's. The first stock is Tyler Corp. It met the rules for the fundamentals: (a) the earnings were up for the last 4 years, and (b) the earnings for the last 4 quarters (the current and the last three) were up.

TYLER CORP

1974=$4.64	4th yearly increase
1973= 3.20	3rd yearly increase
1972= 2.70	2nd yearly increase
1971= 2.54	1st yearly increase
1970= 1.52	

Play It Again, Sam

Barron's reported earnings on May 5, 1975: March 3 months 93 cents versus 86 cents. The previous 3 quarters were:

	1975	1974	1973
Mar. 1st quarter	.93	.86	
June 2nd quarter		1.02	.88
Sept. 3rd quarter		1.72	1.02
Dec. 4th quarter		1.02	.80

These earnings showed that Tyler Corp. was a bonafide growth company.

Tabulated below are the figures as they unfolded week by week in Barron's.

Date	Closing Price	Earnings
1/6/75	14	Sept. 9 Mos. $3.59 vs $2.42
1/13	14-1/2	
1/20	14-3/4	
1/27	14-5/8	
2/3	16-5/8	
2/10	17-5/8	Dec. '74 Earn. $4.63 vs $3.22
2/17	19	
2/24	18-1/8	
3/3	17-1/4	
3/10	18	
3/17	18-1/4	
3/24	18-1/4	
3/31	19	
4/7	18-3/8	
4/14	19-1/8	

Play It Again Sam

Date	Closing Price	Earnings
4/21	19-3/8	
4/28	21	
5/5	23	March 3 Mos. $ .93 vs $ .86
5/12	22-7/8	
5/19	22-1/8	
5/26	21-3/4	Leading indicators give buy signal
6/2	21-1/2	
6/9	22-5/8	
6/16	22-1/8	
6/23	21-7/8	
6/30	22-1/8	
7/7	21-7/8	
7/14	23	
7/21	23-5/8	
7/28	22-1/8	June 6 Mos. $2.33 vs $1.88
8/4	20-3/4	
8/11	19-3/8	
8/18	20-1/8	
8/25	19-5/8	
9/1	20-3/4	
9/8	20-7/8	
9/15	19-3/4	
9/22	19-1/4	
9/29	18-3/4	
10/6	18-1/4	
10/13	19-7/8	
10/20	20-1/4	
10/27	20-1/2	

Play It Again Sam

Date	Closing Price	Earnings
11/3	20-7/8	
11/10	21-1/8	Sept. 9 Mos. $4.10 vs $3.60
11/17	22-1/4	Two for one split announced
11/24	21	
12/1	20-1/2	
12/8	20-1/8	
12/15	19-7/8	
12/22	20	
12/29	20-1/8	
1/5/76	20	
1/12	23-3/8	
1/19	25-5/8	
1/26	26	
2/2	27-1/8	
2/9	28-1/4	
2/16	29	Dec. '75 Earn. $5.52 vs $4.62
2/23	34	
3/1	34-3/4	
3/8	33-3/8	
3/15	34-3/8	
3/22	35-3/4	
3/29	36-3/4	
4/5	36-5/8	
4/12	35-1/2	
4/19	35-3/8	
4/26	34-7/8	
5/3	32-1/2	March 3 Mos. $1.04 vs $ .93
5/10	33-1/4	

Play It Again Sam

Date	Closing Price	Earnings
5/17	33-5/8	
5/24	16-7/8	Two for one split
5/31	18-1/4	
6/7	17	
6/14	17-7/8	
6/21	17-7/8	
6/28	18-1/8	
7/5	19	
7/12	19-1/4	
7/19	19	
7/26	18-1/2	
8/2	19-1/8	June 6 Mos. earn. $1.53 vs $1.17
8/9	20-5/8	
8/16	20-3/8	
8/23	19-1/2	
8/30	18-3/4	
9/6	18-5/8	
9/13	18-3/4	
9/20	19-3/8	
9/27	19-5/8	
10/4	18-3/8	
10/11	17-3/4	
10/18	17-1/4	
10/25	18	
11/1	18-1/2	Sept. 9 Mos. $2.56 vs $2.05
11/8	18-3/4	
11/15	18-5/8	
11/22	20-3/4	

Play It Again Sam

Date	Closing Price	Earnings
11/29	21-7/8	
12/6	22-1/2	
12/13	22-1/4	
12/20	21-3/4	

There is a blank piece of chart paper for you to fill in. As you go along write down the buy and sell signals as well as the commentary.

To refresh your memory, here is how the technical aspect should be handled.

1. Only the weekly closes are plotted. These closing "dots" are connected with straight lines.

2. A buy signal occurs when prices go up, then down, then up again above the preceding peak by at least two points.

3. A sell signal occurs when prices thrust down from the highest point by at least 20%, providing you have a profit. (Do not sell if you can't at least get your round-trip commissions back). If the latest quarterly earnings come out flat or lower, sell even if you have a loss.

If you have sold out at a break-even or a profit, you can buy back the same stock using the same 2 point break-out rule.

If the stock has a dip of 7% or more—but no more than 20%—you can buy more on the first week you get an up-turn.

After having made your chart and written down your comments, check with the chart that follows (Figure 8) and my comments below.

FIGURE 8: Tyler Corp.

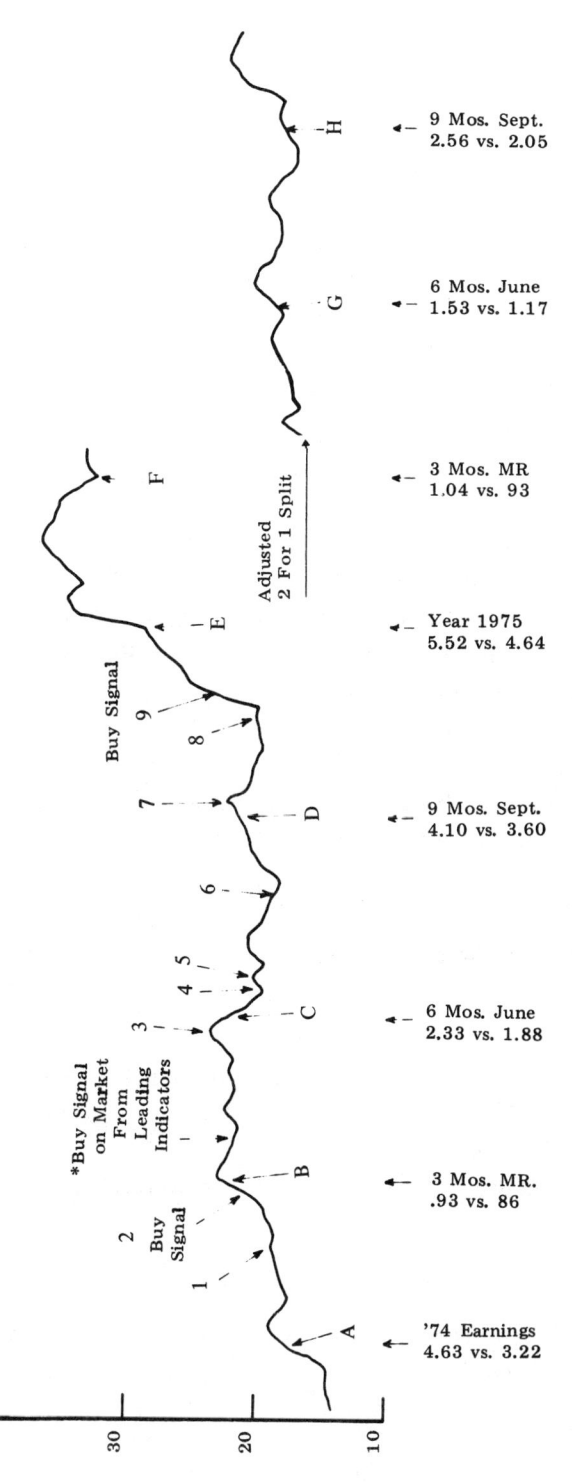

Play It Again Sam

POINT "A"

1974 earnings came in. They were $4.63 vs $4.02. The last quarter, which I haven't given you, were $1.02 vs. $.80.

POINT "2"

This was the buy signal at 21, since the price rose at least 2 points over the bulge at point "1" where the price was 19.

3 months March earnings showed up. They were 93 cents vs. 86 cents, and thus were higher.

**The leading indicators gave a buy signal on May 26, 1975. Since the stock was already bullish we bought on this little pull-back to 21-3/4.

POINT "C"

6 months June earnings came out: $2.33 vs $1.88. Were they higher for the quarter?

6 mos. June	2.33	1.88	
3 mos. Mar.	.93	.86	(Subtract)
	1.40	1.02	

Yes they were so hold the position.

POINT "4"

This dip to 19-1/2 from 23-1/2 (point 3) was 17%. Hold long.

POINT "5"

This up-turn allowed us to buy 100 more at 20-1/4.

Play It Again Sam

POINT "6"

The price dropped to 18-1/2, enough to knock us out. Since this would have given us a loss and since both the leading indicators were bullish and the latest earnings were up, we play to get even. (This means our original investment plus the round-trip commission. We need 21-5/8 to bail out free).

POINT "D" and POINT "7"

New earnings: 9 months Sept. were $4.20 vs $3.60. Were they better for the quarter?

9 mos.Sept.	4.10	3.60	
6 mos.June	2.33	1.88	(Subtract)
	1.77	1.72	

Yes they were. In fact, they pushed the stock up so that we were able to get out at 22-1/4 and thereby even made a little after our commissions.

POINT "9"

Since the leading indicators and the fundamentals were bullish, we take another shot at the stock. We buy 100 shares at 23-3/4 (point "9") since this exceeded by 2 points the bulge at point "8" (20-1/8).

Twelve months earnings appear in the Barron's: $5.52 vs $4.64. How did they compare for the last quarter?

12 mos.Dec.	5.52	4.64	
9 mos.Sept.	4.10	3.60	(Subtract)
	1.42	1.04	

Play It Again Sam

POINT "F"

3 months earnings are printed: $1.04 vs $.93. Hold. Then a 2 for 1 split is announced.

POINT "G"

6 months earnings show up: $1.53 vs $1.17. How good were they?

6 mos. June	1.53	1.17	
3 mos. Mar.	1.04	.93	(Subtract)
	.49	.24	

That's a hundred percent increase!

POINT "H"

Earnings again:

9 mos. Sept.	2.56	2.05	
6 mos. June	1.53	1.17	(Subtract)
	1.03	.88	

These are better, so stay long.

If we had sold the stock on the week our data ends, we would have gotten 21-3/4. Since we held 200 shares because of the 2 for 1 split, we would have grossed $4350. With our cost at $2375, we made a profit of $1975, or 83%.

Remember, the market doesn't know that your first purchase didn't work out for you. You should also not look back. Try to act, the second time around, as if you were making a brand new commitment. You see how well it worked out!

Play It Again Sam

Let's try a second one. This time it'll be Universal Leaf as shown in Figure 9.

The last four years and the last four quarters were higher so the company was growing.

Recorded below are all the prices and earnings as they appeared in Barron's every week.

Date	Closing Price	Earnings
1/6/75	26-3/8	
1/13	27	
1/20	27-3/8	
1/27	27	
2/3	28-1/2	
2/10	30	Dec. 6 mos. $3.16 vs $2.74
2/17	32-1/2	
2/24	32-3/8	
3/3	31-3/4	
3/10	31-7/8	
3/17	33-1/4	
3/24	33	
3/31	35	
4/7	35-1/4	
4/14	35-1/2	
4/21	35-5/8	
4/28	36	
5/5	36-5/8	Mar. 9 mos. $5.24 vs $4.42
5/12	38-1/8	
5/19	37-3/4	
5/26	38-1/4	Leading indicators give buy signal

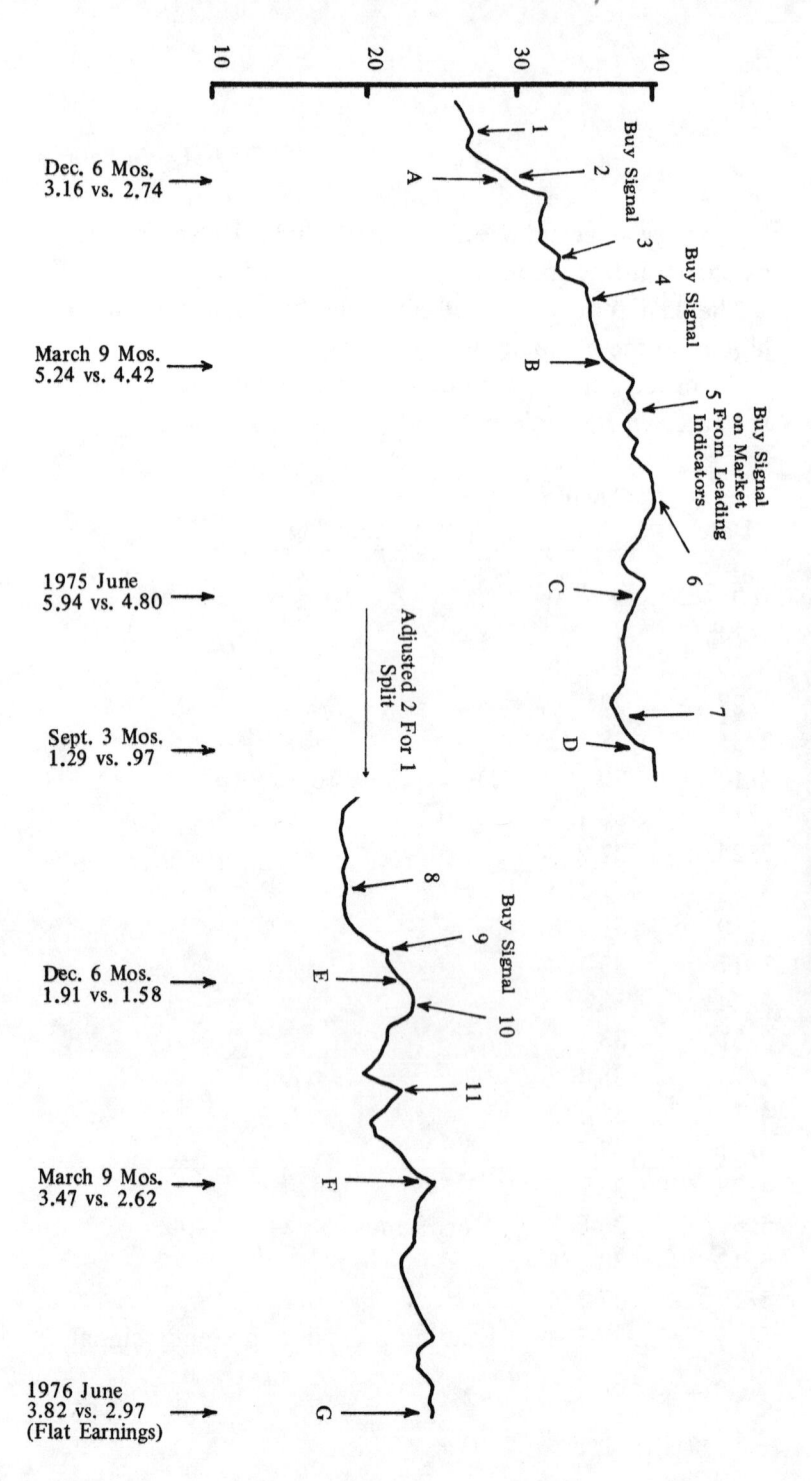

FIGURE 9: Universal Leaf Tobacco

Play It Again Sam

Date	Closing Price	Earnings
6/2	37-1/4	
6/9	38-5/8	
6/16	38	
6/23	39-1/8	
6/30	39-1/2	
7/7	39-3/4	
7/14	39	
7/21	38-7/8	
7/28	38	
8/4	37-3/8	
8/11	39	
8/18	38-1/2	June '75 $5.94 vs $4.80
8/25	38	
9/1	37-1/2	
9/8	37-1/2	
9/15	37-3/8	
9/22	37-1/2	
9/29	37-1/4	
10/6	36-5/8	
10/13	37	
10/20	37-3/4	
10/27	39-5/8	Sept. 3 mos. $1.29 vs $ .97
11/3	39-5/8	
11/10	39-7/8	
11/17	19-7/8	Two for one split
11/24	18-1/2	
12/1	18-1/2	
12/8	18-3/4	

Play It Again Sam

Date	Closing Price	Earnings
12/15	19	
12/22	18-3/4	
12/29	19	
1/5/76	18-3/4	
1/12	19	
1/19	20	
1/26	21-3/4	
2/2	21-1/2	
2/9	23	Dec. 6 mos. $1.91 vs $1.58
2/16	23-1/2	
2/23	23-1/4	
3/1	21-1/2	
3/8	21-3/8	
3/15	21	
3/22	20	
3/29	22-3/8	
4/5	21-3/4	
4/12	20-1/2	
4/19	20-7/8	
4/26	22-1/8	
5/3	23	
5/10	25	Mar. 9 mos. $3.47 vs $2.62
5/17	24	
5/24	23-5/8	
5/31	23-1/4	
6/7	23-1/4	
6/14	22-5/8	
6/21	22-7/8	
6/28	23	

Play It Again Sam

Date	Closing Price	Earnings
7/5	23-3/8	
7/12	24	
7/19	24-3/4	
7/26	23-3/4	
8/2	23-5/8	
8/9	24-3/4	
8/16	24-3/8	
8/23	24-1/2	June '76 $3.82 vs $2.97

POINT "5," POINT "A," POINT "B"

The leading indicators gave a buy signal. What did the stock look like?

First: the earnings met our rules for the previous four years.

1974 = $4.80	4th yearly increase
1973 = 4.02	3rd yearly increase
1972 = 3.56	2nd yearly increase
1971 = 3.38	1st yearly increase
1970 = 3.06	

Second: the last four quarters were higher.

	1974	1973	1972
Sept. quarter	.98	.92	
Dec. quarter	2.18	1.82	
Mar. quarter	2.08	1.68	
June quarter		.38	def. .01

Play It Again Sam

You can see them trending upwards from the chart notations where I have marked them.

POINT "1," POINT "2," POINT "3," POINT "4"

The stock had already given two buy signals before the leading indicators said to go ahead and buy. Point "2" exceeded point "1" by at least two points and point "4" exceeded point "3" by at least two points. So at point "5", where the leading indicators gave a buy signal, we purchase 100 shares at 38-1/8.

POINT "C"

The year's earnings came out in Barron's: $5.94 vs $4.80. How did these stack up?

12 mos. June	5.94	4.80	
9 mos. Mar.	5.24	4.42	(Subtract)
	.70	.38	

That's a good increase.

POINT "7"

There was an 8% dip—from 39-3/4 (point "6") to 36-1/2 (the week before point "7").

We buy another 100 shares at 37 (point "7") because this is the first up-turn after the dip. At this point we are long 100 at 38-1/8 and another 100 at 37.

POINT "D"

New first quarter earnings: $1.29 vs $ .97. Fine, hold. Also notice that the stock will be split two for one and that

Play It Again Sam

this will happen three weeks after point "D."

POINT "9"

Another buy signal occurs here if you want to increase your position, since the price rose at least two points higher than the bulge at point "8." Since we have 200 shares, we'll just stay pat.

POINT "E"

Another earnings report: December 6 months were $1.91 vs $1.58. How were these?

Dec. 6 mos.	1.91	1.58	
*Sept.3 mos.	.65	.49	(Subtract)
	1.26	1.09	

*Don't forget to adjust the old first quarter earnings to account for the two for one split. The "old first quarter earnings were $1.29 versus $.97. The split makes them $.65 versus $.49 (the half cents are rounded up to the nearest cent).

The week before point "11" there was a dip of 14% from 23-1/4 (point "10") to 20. Point "11" is the first up-turn so we bought another 200 shares at 22-1/2. (We bought 200 instead of 100 shares because this purchase is the equivalent of 100 of the pre-split shares). This gives us three positions. Because of the two for one split, we are long 200 shares at 37, another 200 at 38-1/8, and the 200 we just bought at 22-1/2.

POINT "F"

Another earnings report: March 9 months were $3.47 as

Play It Again Sam

against $2.62. How were these?

Mar. 9 mos.	3.47	2.82	
Dec. 6 mos.	1.91	1.58	(Subtract)
	1.56	1.24	

They're still marching up like good soldiers.

POINT "G"

Again earnings: 1976 June were $3.82 versus $2.97. Are they still going higher?

June 12 mos.	3.82	2.97	
Mar. 9 mos.	3.47	2.62	(Subtract)
	.35	.35	

No, the earnings were "flat." So we have to sell out at 24-1/2.

How'd we come out? We sold 600 shares at 24-1/2, which comes to $14,700.

```
We bought 100 at 37 which came to        $ 3700
We bought 100 at 38-1/8 which came to      3812
We bought 200 at 22-1/2 which came to      4500
                       Total cost        $12,012

    Sold 600 for      $14700
    Bought 600 for     12012  (subtract)
                      $ 2688  (gross profit)
```

Play It Again Sam

This was a 22% gain on our original capital of $12,012. If 50% margin were used, all the quantities would have been doubled, including the profits. They would have shot up from 22% to 44%.

In this chapter you have reinforced your understanding of how to use the fundamentals and the price movements of a growth company. Don't hesitate to practice some more by going to the library and working out of the tear sheets and Barron's. You can buy the chart paper in any variety store. The more you practice, the easier and greater your profits will be.

CHAPTER 6

ETCETERA, ETCETERA, ETCETERA—
Or How To Track Additional Growth Stocks

Just as you look for new clothes to buy, so you should be on the look-out for additional investments. There is always something new popping up. How do you stay on top of it?

Very easily, if you use Barron's. Every week, as has been pointed out, new earnings are published. If any freshly reported earnings are up, pull the tearsheet and analyze them as before. If the "fundamentals" say buy, then work up the chart.

SOME ILLUSTRATIONS

Olin Corp. came out in Barron's with new earnings for six months ending June. (This is point "B" on the chart). After pulling out the tear sheet, I first of all saw that this was a relatively new company as far as the NYSE went.

Etcetera, Etcetera, Etcetera

The graph on the front of the tear sheet shows it was admitted to trading in the second quarter of 1974.

A check on the yearly earnings on the back of the tear sheet showed these yearly earnings:

1974 = $4.10	4th yearly increase
1973 = 2.25	3rd yearly increase
1972 = 1.37	2nd yearly increase
1971 = 1.24	1st yearly increase
1970 = 1.18	

The last 4 quarters were also higher:

	1975	1974	1973
Mar. quarter	1.38	1.03	
June quarter	1.70	1.47	
(6 mos. as given in Barron's)	3.08	2.50	
Sept. quarter		1.04	.52
Dec. quarter		.56	.31

As you can see in Figure 10, to check the last 4 quarters (since I only had two quarters from Barron's) I had to use the last two quarters of Sept. and Dec. as taken from the tear sheet.

POINT "A"

Since the earnings said "buy," I then constructed a chart starting with May, 1975, the week the leading indicators gave a buy signal.

FIGURE 10: Olin Corp.

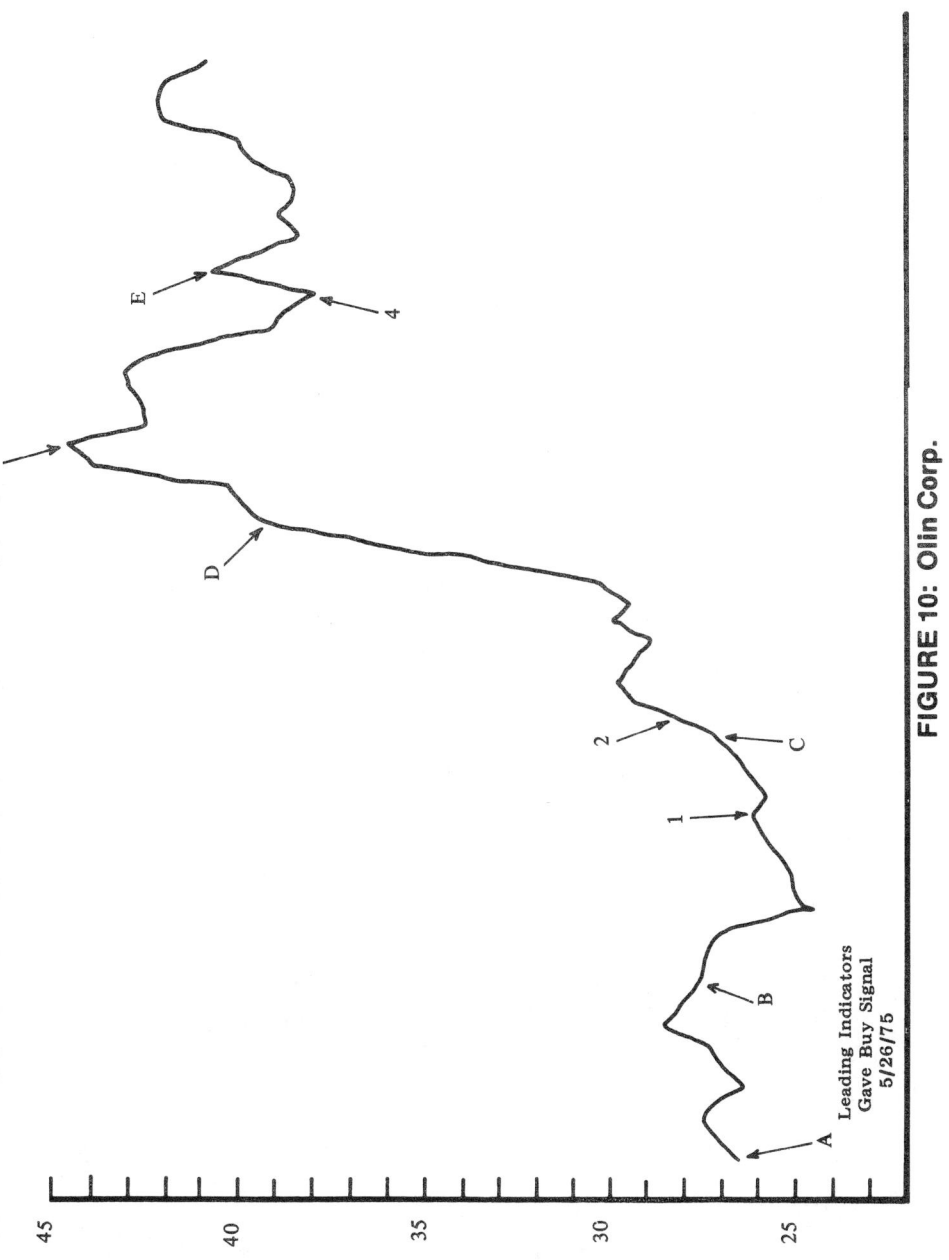

Etcetera, Etcetera, Etcetera

POINT "B"
These were those six months earnings that were just analyzed, and they were good.

POINT "C"
Nine months earnings came out: $4.34 versus $3.54. Were they higher for the quarter?

3rd quarter	4.34	3.54	
2nd quarter	3.08	2.50	(Subtract)
	1.26	1.04	

Fine earnings, but, unfortunately, no chart buy.

POINT "2"
Here is where we get a "minor trend break-out" at 28. This was two points above the bulge at point "1" (price was 26).

POINT "D"
Twelve months earnings: $5.03 versus $4.10. They must be broken down.

4th quarter	5.03	4.10	
3rd quarter	4.34	3.54	(Subtract)
	.69	.56	

So far, so good. Olin is bullish and the earnings are up.

POINT "4"
After swirling to a high of 44-3/8 (point "3"), the price

Etcetera, Etcetera, Etcetera

retreated to 38-5/8 (point "4"). Was this enough to get us out, to trigger our "20% dip rule?" Since this retracement was only 13% all we had was heart burn.

POINT "E"

New first quarter earnings appeared: $1.72 versus $1.38. Hold your long position.

When the chart stops, Olin is 40-5/8. Since it was bought for 28, the gross profit was about 12-1/2 points, or 45%.

SUPER VALUE

Here's another stock, charted on Figure 11, that came along after the leading indicators gave a "bull" signal on May 26, 1975.

POINT "A"

The first quarter earnings came out at $.82 versus $.69 for June. At this point both 4 year and 4 quarter earnings had to be checked. This is how they stacked up.

These are the 4 year earnings:

1974 = $2.88	4th yearly increase
1973 = 2.38	3rd yearly increase
1972 = 2.20	2nd yearly increase
1971 = 2.08	1st yearly increase
1970 = 1.52	

The last 4 quarters were also higher:

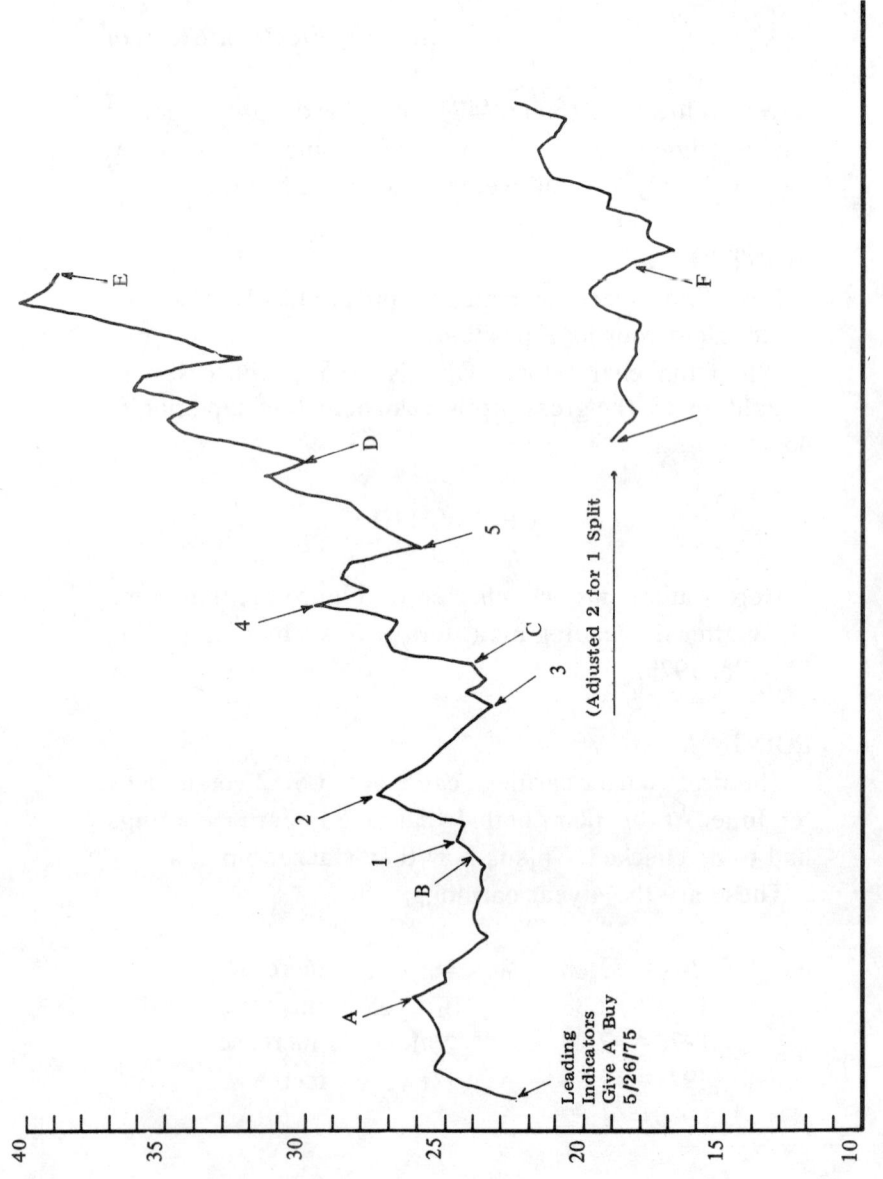

FIGURE 11: Super Value

Etcetera, Etcetera, Etcetera

	1975	1974	1973
1st quarter June	.82	.69	
2nd quarter Sept.		.70	.46
3rd quarter Dec.		.72	.60
4th quarter Feb.		.76	.64

Notice how I had to go back to the tear sheet in order to check on the earnings for the previous three quarters.

POINT "B"

Six months earnings are in: $1.69 versus $1.39. Are they better?

2nd quarter	1.69	1.39	
1st quarter	.82	.69	(Subtract)
	.87	.70	

The earnings are higher, but the stock isn't. Don't buy, wait.

POINT "2"

This is where we get a buy signal—price 27-3/8. Since this exceeds our "2 point break-out rule" everything says go long.

POINT "3"

We no sooner get our buy than we get shot down. Prices skid to 23-1/2. This will tell if you're made of "true grit." But by sticking to our rules, we're still hanging in. The cave-in to 23-1/2 was 15%, not enough to clip us.

Etcetera, Etcetera, Etcetera

POINT "C"

Nine months earnings were printed in Barron's: $2.59 versus $2.11.

3rd quarter	2.59	2.11	
2nd quarter	1.69	1.39	(Subtract)
	.90	.72	

Beautiful! These are good enough to make the price jump.

POINT "5"

Another bounce off of the high. The retracement was only 13%, so we are still long.

POINT "D"

Twelve months earnings were $3.60 versus $2.88.

4th quarter	3.60	2.88	
3rd quarter	2.59	2.11	(Subtract)
	1.01	.77	

That's a smart increase.

POINT "E"

First quarter earnings are in: $1.25 versus $.82. Another sharp increase. Ride the wave.

POINT "6"

Super Value announced a two for one split. This meant that for every 100 shares you had you now are the proud

Etcetera, Etcetera, Etcetera

owner of two hundred. But...and there is a "but" here, since no one is going to give you anything for nothing, the price of the stock is sliced in half. You still have the same size baloney, only now it's in two pieces.

You can see that the new scale was drawn reflecting the split and was placed at a comparable level to the old scale.

POINT "F"

New six month's earnings: $1.16 versus $.85.

2nd quarter	1.16	.85	
1st quarter	.62	.41	(Subtract)
	.54	.44	(Adjusted for a 2 for 1 split).

As they say: "Maintain a positive stance."

At the close of the chart, the price was 22-3/4. How much did we gross? One hundred shares originally cost us about $2750 (100 times $27.50). The two hundred shares we now own are worth $4550 (200 times 22-3/4). The gross profit was $1800 or 65%.

Let's look at some later examples that flashed a buy during 1977.

Abbott Labs has been a fine growth company (See Figure 12). Its earnings for the previous 4 years looked like this:

1975 = 2.57	4th yearly increase
1974 = 2.00	3rd yearly increase
1973 = 1.68	2nd yearly increase
1972 = 1.44	1st yearly increase
1971 = .86	

113

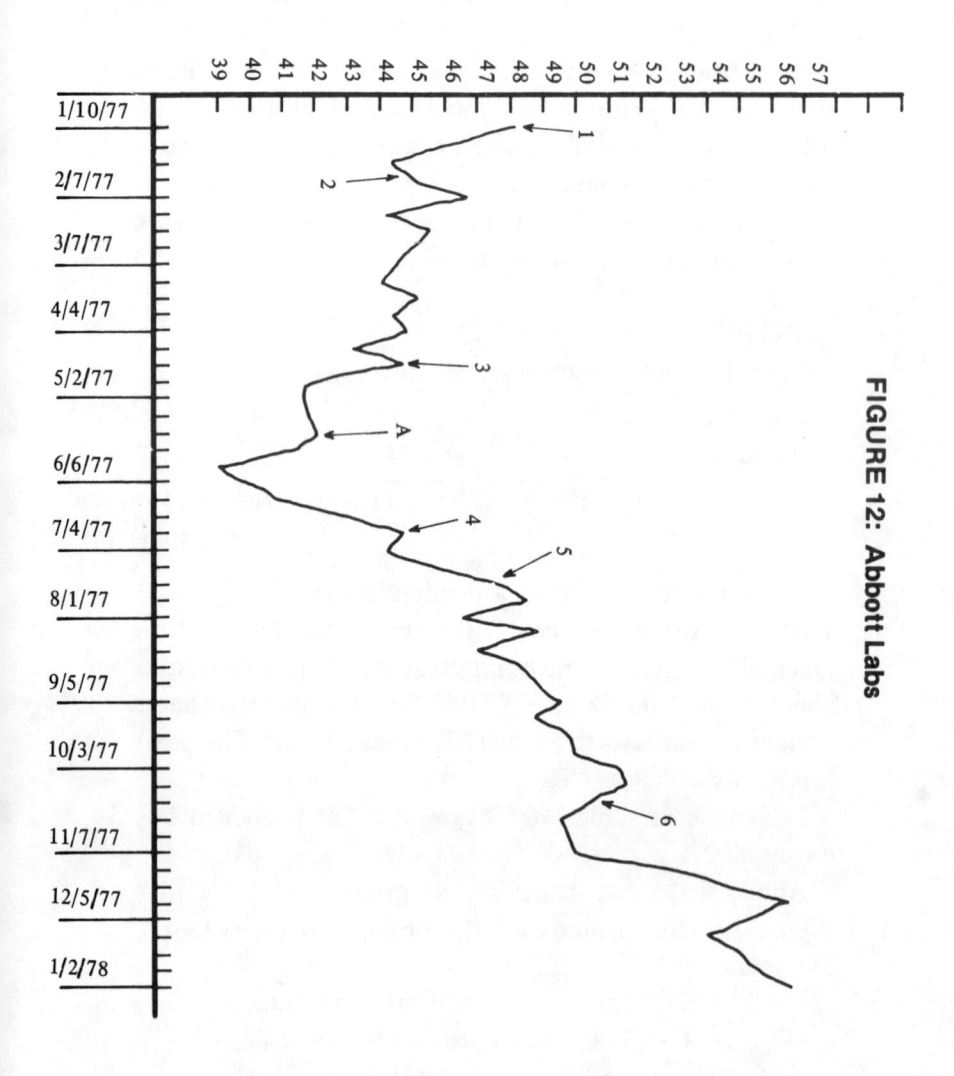

FIGURE 12: Abbott Labs

Etcetera, Etcetera, Etcetera

The previous 4 quarters spelled growth also and looked like this:

	1976	1975	1974
1st quarter Mar.	.72	.57	
2nd quarter June	.76	.57	
3rd quarter Sept.	.76	.60	
4th quarter Dec.		.83	.62

Here's what happened as we ground out the earnings and weekly closes from Barron's...

POINT "1"

On January 10, 1977, Abbott Labs was 47-5/8 and the earnings for Sept., 1976 were 76 cents versus 60 cents for the corresponding quarter. The fundamentals were fine. All that was needed was a buy signal on the chart.

POINT "2"

The new December earnings showed up in Barron's. They were for the year and were $3.66 versus $2.35. Were they higher or did they mask a decrease? Let's see...

4th quarter	3.26	2.57	
3rd quarter	2.24	1.74	(Subtract)
	1.02	.83	

POINT "3"

New earnings appeared in Barron's. For the first quarter of March, they were 85 cents versus 72 cents. So the earnings are still growing. Keep in mind, however, that we have not yet bought the stock.

Etcetera, Etcetera, Etcetera

POINT "4"

Here's where we buy it—at 44-5/8, because the price is now at least 2 points higher than the last high at point "A" (42).

POINT "5"

New earnings are given: for 6 months June they were $1.79 versus $1.48. Were they better?

2nd quarter	1.79	1.48	
1st quarter	.85	.72	(Subtract)
	.93	.76	

That's what we want—better earnings!

POINT "6"

New earnings again. This time for 9 months Sept. Here's how they stacked up...

3rd quarter	2.72	2.24	
2nd quarter	1.79	1.48	(Subtract)
	.93	.76	

Still going great!

As of the beginning of 1978, we were still in the stock and the price was 56-1/2, right on the high of the move!

How much profit did we make on Abbott Labs if we had sold it? Let's see...

Etcetera, Etcetera, Etcetera

```
Sold 100 at 56-1/2    = $5650.00
Bought 100 at 44-5/8 =   4462.50  (Subtract)
Gross Profit            $1187.50
```

That comes to 21% on our investment.

I became interested in Church's Fried Chicken in November, 1976, the same month in which the New York Stock Exchange admitted the stock for trading. Even before they traded on the "Big Board," however, Church's showed consistent earnings gains. Let's use our technique to follow Church's stock through 1977 (See Figure 13).

4 year earnings were strong:

1975 =	$2.36	4th yearly increase
1974 =	1.91	3rd yearly increase
1973 =	1.05	2nd yearly increase
1972 =	1.01	1st yearly increase
1971 =	.98	

The previous 4 quarters looked just as good:

	1976	1975	1974
1st quarter Mar.	.59	.36	
2nd quarter June	.87	.53	
3rd quarter Sept.	.96	.62	
4th quarter Dec.		.84	.50

Now we're ready to follow the weekly closes reported in

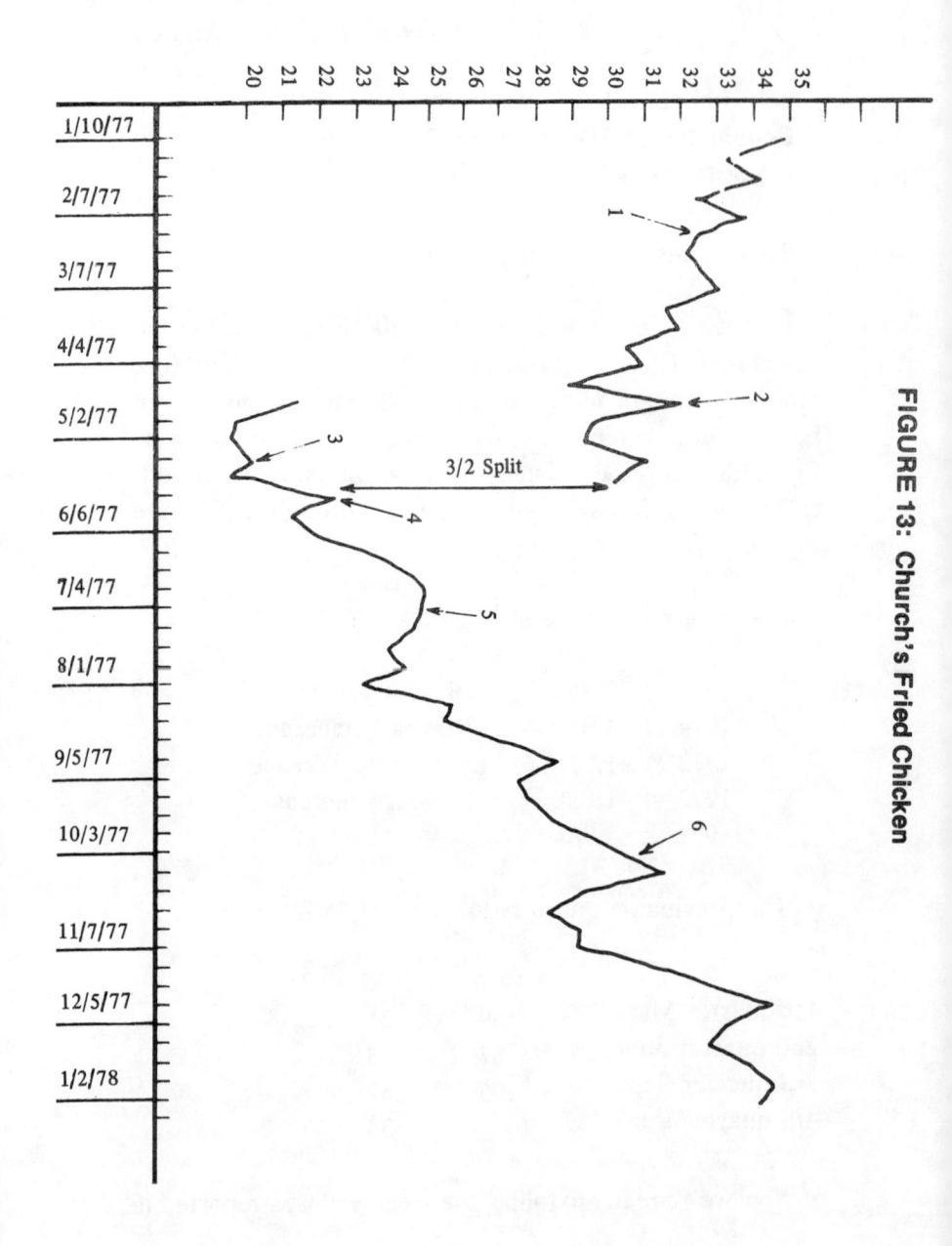

FIGURE 13: Church's Fried Chicken

Etcetera, Etcetera, Etcetera

Barron's...

Church's Fried Chicken on Jan. 10, 1977, was at 34-7/8. 3rd quarter Sept. earnings were 96 cents versus 62 cents, a big 55% increase. The company looked good, but we wait for the buy signal.

POINT "1"

Yearly earnings were reported in Barron's, so we check for an increase...

4th quarter.	3.66	2.35	
3rd quarter	2.42	1.51	(Subtract)
	1.24	.84	

Still looks good!

POINT "2"

First quarter earnings from Barron's—82 cents versus 59 cents. Hang on for the buy signal!

On May 24, Church's Fried Chicken made a 3/2 split, also known as a 50% stock dividend. Each shareholder received 1 extra share for every 2 he held. But the price of the stock must be adjusted downward, since three shares of the stock after the split are worth the same as two shares before the split. Your newspaper will follow the stock that is about to be split (splits must be approved by the stockholders) and list two prices, the current pre-split price, and the "when issued" price ("when issued" means adjusted for the split).

The split affects earnings, too, since earnings are stated per share. With more shares, earnings must also be

119

Etcetera, Etcetera, Etcetera

adjusted downward for all quarters. But don't forget, we're comparing earnings of corresponding quarters. Let's revise the earnings for the split...

	1977	1976	1975
1st quarter Mar.	.55	.39	
2nd quarter June		.58	.35
3rd quarter Sept.		.64	.41
4th quarter Dec.		.83	.56

The split stock is valued at 2/3 of the pre-split stock. So, to revalue earnings, simply multiply each earnings figure by 2/3. We've adjusted for a split on the chart and are now ready for our first buy signal.

POINT "4"

May 23, Church's closed at 22-3/8. Since we're looking for at least a 2 dollar rise above the previous high, which was Point "3" where the price is 20-1/8,—we have our buy point and we make our purchase.

POINT "5"

Barron's reported 2nd quarter June earnings, $1.32 against 97 cents. How's our stock doing?

2nd quarter	1.32	.97	
1st quarter	.55	.39	(Subtract)
	.77	.58	

Still going strong!

Etcetera, Etcetera, Etcetera

POINT "6"

3rd quarter earnings reported in Barron's, $2.19 versus $1.61. Are the earnings up for the quarter?

3rd quarter	2.19	1.61	
2nd quarter	1.32	.97	(Subtract)
	.87	.64	

Yes, the earnings are up. In fact, we hang on right through Jan. 2, 1978, when the price is 34-3/8!

Here's how we figure our profit if we had sold out at 34-3/8. We bought 100 at 22-3/8 and sold 100 at 34-3/8 for a 12 point gross profit, or $1200. This is a big 53% on our capital!

Like Church's Fried Chicken, Datapoint Corporation is a newcomer to the "Big Board." (See Figure 14). Sometimes keeping an eye opened to these new stocks can give the investor good leads. Let's look at Datapoint's earnings:

1975 = 2.56	4th yearly increase
1974 = 2.02	3rd yearly increase
1973 = 1.65	2nd yearly increase
1972 = 1.27	1st yearly increase
1971 = .68	

The last four quarters also showed fine growth:

	1976	1975	1974
1st quarter Oct.	.60	.38	
2nd quarter Jan.	.65	.51	
3rd quarter Apr.		.54	.39
4th quarter July		.57	.50

FIGURE 14: Datapoint Corp.

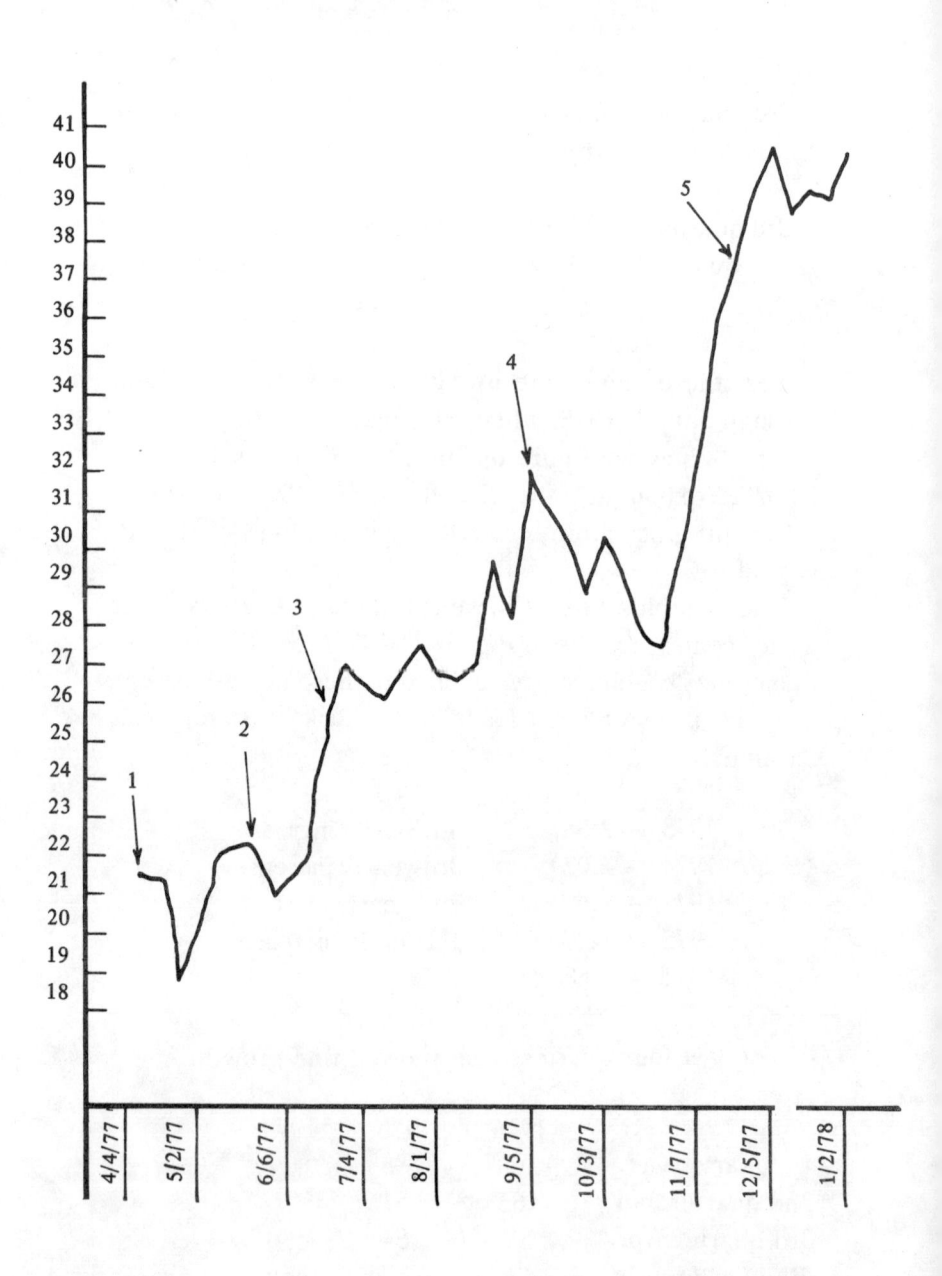

Etcetera, Etcetera, Etcetera

POINT "1"

Datapoint began trading on the New York Stock Exchange in April, 1977. 2nd quarter January earnings were 65 cents versus 51 cents and the price was 21-1/2.

POINT "2"

3rd quarter April earnings reported in Barron's—$1.84 versus $1.44. What do the earnings tell us?

3rd quarter	1.84	1.44	
2nd quarter	1.25	.89	(Subtract)
	.59	.55	

Keep looking for the buy signal!

POINT "3"

Datapoint is 25-5/8, more than 2 points over the last high at Point "2" (22-1/4). That tells us to buy.

POINT "4"

Yearly earnings reported in Barron's, $2.56 versus $2.02. Is that good news for us?

4th quarter	2.56	2.02	
3rd quarter	1.84	1.44	(Subtract)
	.72	.58	

It certainly is!

POINT "5"

First quarter earnings reported in Barron's, 85 cents

Etcetera, Etcetera, Etcetera

versus 60 cents. *Datapoint is still doing very well.*

On January 2, 1978, the price was 40-1/4 and we were still in our position. But let's figure out our profits if we had sold out...

```
Sold 100 at 40-1/4    = $4025.00
Bought 100 at 25-5/8  =  2562.50
Gross Profit            $1462.50
```

That's 36% on our money!

HOW TO BUY A GROWTH-ORIENTED MUTUAL FUND

It may have occurred to some of you that instead of buying individual growth companies, you should, instead, buy a mutual fund that specializes in growth stocks. In this way you don't have to worry about keeping up with the earnings. All you have to do is keep plotting the chart.

Such a growth fund is Price T. Rowe's Growth Fund, plotted on Figure 15. It is listed in Barron's in the section on mutual funds. The actual listing is "Price (Rowe) Growth." The fund is a no load, which means that there is no fee for buying it or selling it.

POINT "2"

There was a buy signal at 10.35, a half a dollar over the last hump at #1 (9.85). For a mutual fund at such a low price, our buying rule is modified: instead of using one

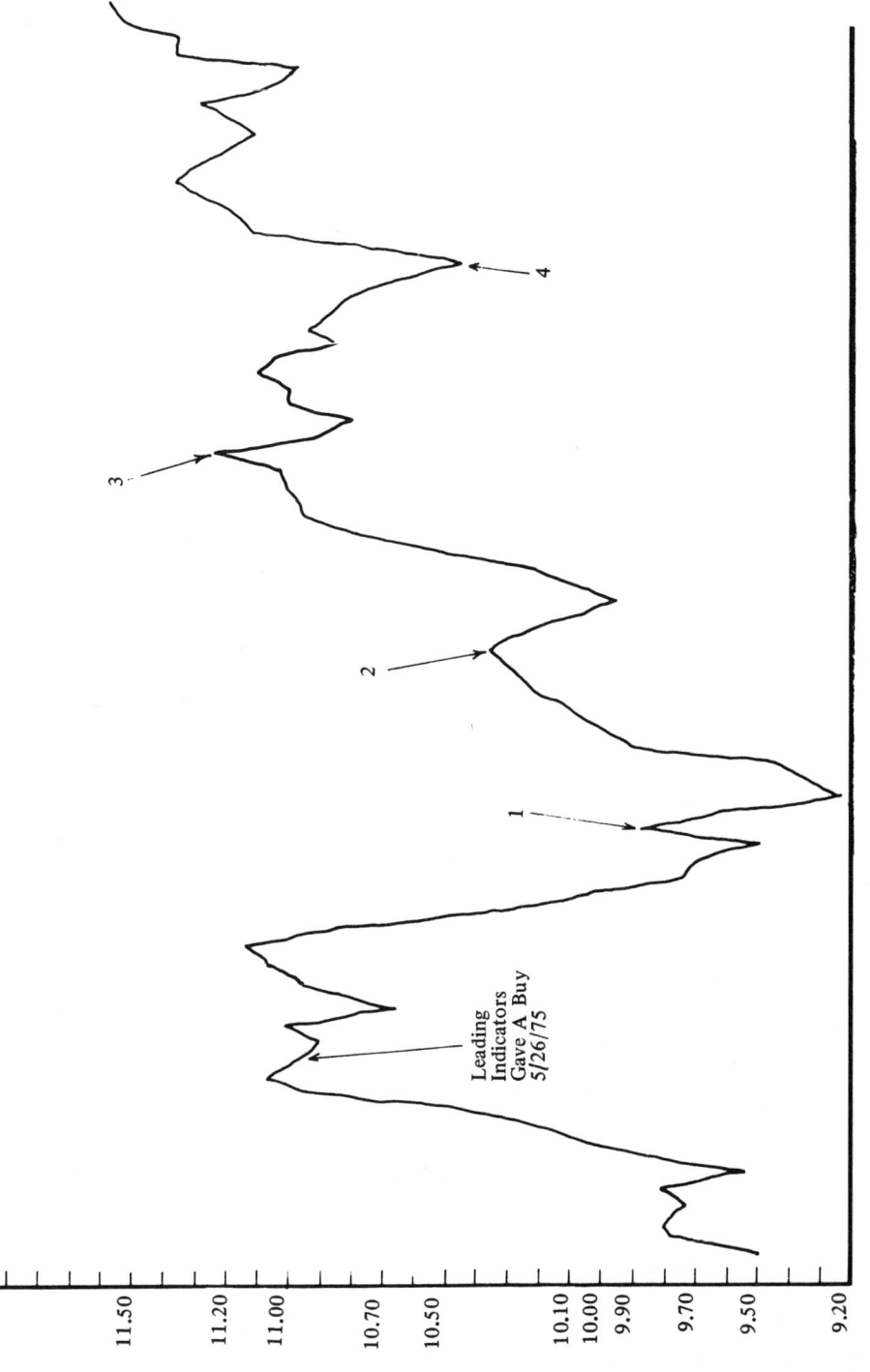

FIGURE 15: Price [Rowe] Growth

Etcetera, Etcetera, Etcetera

point for the break-out, only one-half point is used.

POINT "4"

This dip looks serious, but is it? From the high of 11.21 to the drop at 10.43 is only a little over 9%, so our 20% dip rule keeps us in.

At the end of the chart the price was 11.55. How much gross profit was made? The gross profit was 1.20 per share, or about 11%.

CHAPTER 7

FOR MATHEMATICIANS ONLY—
Or How To Pick A Growth Stock That's Undervalued

There are some people who get their kicks from doing mental work, particularly mathematics. Unfortunately, the study and use of mathematics is difficult. The thread that has to be followed that leads from Euclid's plane geometry through Descarte's analytic geometry to Newton's calculus demands clever minds. In this case, the shortest path is far from a straight line.

THE IMPORTANCE OF MATHEMATICS

Using mathematics in any field is very important. Just look about you, on you and in you, and you can see that mathematics has contributed greatly to your well being.

For Mathematicians Only

Without it, builders would still be digging out caves, heat would be furnished with logs, light would glow from candles, clothes would be made from skins, hands would be cleaned by wiping on leaves, and doctors would care by leeching. In short, we would have none of the benefits and marvels of our "mathematical civilization."

Being an egghead does not mean being impractical. Because one uses his brains does not mean he cannot make money. One of the first philosophers of western civiilization was an ancient Greek by the name of Thales. In fact, he was one of the Seven Wise Men of Greece, and it is thought that western philosophy starts with him. Aristotle, a giant of a philosopher who lived about 250 years later, tells this story of Thales in his book, "Politics." I will paraphrase it.

Thales was criticized by his friends, even made fun of by them, for his poverty. What good is your philosophy, they laughed, if you're always broke? They knew that Thales had travelled to many parts of the civilized world. In Egypt he picked up enough geometry to calculate the distance of a ship at sea from observations taken at two points on land and how to estimate the height of a pyramid from the length of its shadow. In Babylonia, he learned how to predict eclipses and other natural results from this "star science."

What his friends and detractors did not know was that because of his skill in the stars, Thales, while it was still winter, predicted that there would be a great harvest of olives in the coming year. This was his secret and he was going to use it to the hilt.

With the little bit of money that he had, he went to his

For Mathematicians Only

own city, Miletus, and the nearby town of Chios. He gave deposits to use all of the olive presses for himself. No one bid against him because it was way before harvest time—remember it was still winter—and no one ever dreamed of the huge olive harvest that was to come. When the avalanche of olives arrived, everyone wanted the presses all at once. Thales let them have them at any rate he pleased, and made a barrel of money.

Today, he would have been said to have "cornered the market" and "made a killing." Thales said that this proves to the world that philosophers "can easily be rich if they like, but that their ambition is of another sort."

Like Thales, we are going to use "the queen of the sciences" to see if we can't improve our chances of making money in the stock market.

WHY MATHEMATICS IS USED IN STOCK ANALYSIS

The art of security analysis might be said to be that of choosing the right stock at the wrong time. We are going to reverse that witticism and choose the right stock at the right time.

Our previous rules of buying only growth stocks and timing their purchases and sales by using the "weekly minor trend" rule does this for us. But we have a very practical problem. Since our investment funds are limited, just how do we go about narrowing down the list of possibilities? In short, how do we mathematically decide which are the most undervalued growth stocks, and, therefore, which are the cheapest to buy?

This propels us into the very theory of why stock prices go up and down. And it involves the mathematics of growth—*compound interest*.

Before World War II, much of security analysis dealt with calculating whether the assets of a company were enough to insure the safety of that company's dividend. Stocks were bought, not so much for the capital gain, but for the greater return they paid over bonds or bank savings. As a single figure, book value was considered an important indication of stock price value. It was felt that as book value rose, the security of the dividend payment increased. It was of prime importance that the dividend be safe. Stocks were bought either because they paid better income than other investments or were regarded as good speculations. They were hardly ever considered as growth investments. Companies wanting to create the greatest attraction for their stocks sometimes used "creative" bookkeeping to overstate their assets. There were plenty of incidents of watered balance sheets where assets were fraudulently overstated.

After the Second World War, however, the income side of the balance sheet became more important. With continuing inflation and rising interest rates, bonds as a way of preserving capital became less attractive. There was a more secure and growing economy. Improvements in accounting made the income statements of corporations more reliable. These led to the recognition that investment in common stocks would not only provide income, but also *growth in the original capital*.

A new approach was developed. Today, the income

For Mathematicians Only

statement receives most of the attention of the securities analyst and the *trend in earnings is regarded as the principal determinant of stock value.*

(As before, with the asset side of the balance sheet, we now have some companies "manipulating" the income side in order to create apparent growth in the earnings per share).

When evaluation moved from the assets, book value, and dividends to the trend in earnings per share, some method had to be found for comparing these different trends to see which company's earnings were growing the fastest and, therefore, which were the best to buy. The most widely used method is a *discounting of anticipated future earnings over a certain number of years.*

THE MATHEMATICS OF COMPOUND INTEREST

The mathematics needed to do this are those based on compound interest. The power of compound interest is like the force of an atom bomb to a ton of dynamite. Our own Ben Franklin well illustrated this potential. Back in 1783, when Ben was 83, he added a section to his will. He set up a codicil that was to last for 200 years after his death. He allotted $5000 each to Boston and Philadelphia. The money was to provide loans to needy young people. The borrowers were required to pay back the loans at 5% interest over 10-year periods.

Each city's fund, according to Ben's will, was to be operated for 200 years. After 100 years, Boston and Philadelphia could each withdraw $500,000 from their

For Mathematicians Only

funds and use the money for public works. The rest was to be left until 1991. At that time the cities could use the money for any purpose.

Now $5000 may not seem like a lot today, but stop and think. What do you guess the value of each fund will be by 1991? Remember that compound interest begins to work in earnest over the last 100 years. In 1991, each fund will be worth more than $20,000,000! That's right: Ben's $5000 grows in 200 years to over $20 million because of the power of compound interest.

Ben Franklin, the first authentic genius of the United States, might have become one of the greatest financiers our country ever produced if stock markets had existed in his day.

One method that has been very useful is to project earnings out eleven years (usually ten years are used, but eleven years works out better). A growth rate for the earnings is assumed. Then the earnings for each year are added up. If the current price of the stock is lower than these projected total earnings, the stock is undervalued and should be bought.

Let's take an example. Suppose a company earns $1.00 a share this year and has been increasing its earnings compounded at 10% a year. How much will it earn at the end of eleven years if the earnings for each year are added together?

Before we can compute this we must know how compound interest is figured. The best way is to start with simple interest, as you would with a savings account.

Suppose you put $500 in your savings account on which the bank will pay you 5%. How much interest will you

For Mathematicians Only

receive by the end of the first year? How much will your total savings be?

Since percent means part of a hundred, we must change the 5% to hundredths. This is done by making a fraction: 5/100.

This fraction is then changed to a decimal, like this:

$$5/100 = 5.00 \div 100 = .05$$

This decimal, .05 is then multiplied by the $500.

$$\$500 \times .05 = \$25.00$$

So the answer is $25 interest. It's called "simple" interest, because the figuring is only on the principal, and simple to do. The total savings will be $500 plus $25, or $525.

Let's extend this example. Suppose you decide to reinvest the total for one more year. How much will you end up with at the end of two years? This is where *compound interest* comes into play.

The second year's interest is not figured on the original $500, but on the principal plus the accumulated interest. In this case it's $525.

Here's the mathematics of the second year:

$$\$525 \times .05 = \$26.25$$

At the end of the second year, the interest paid is $26.25. Notice that, because of the compounding, the interest paid at the end of the second year amounts to

For Mathematicians Only

$1.25 more than at the end of the first year. This will continue to increase each year because of continual building of the interest increments.

At the end of the second year, the total amount you would have would be $551.25.

$$\$525.00 + \$26.25 = \$551.25$$

Now let's go back to our original problem. Suppose a company earns $1.00 a share this year and has been increasing its earnings at 10% compounded rate. How much will it earn at the end of eleven years if the earnings for each year are added together.

Year 1

```
$1.00            1.00
 x.10           +.10
 .1000 = $.10 interest   1.10  amount at end of year 1
```

Year 2

```
$1.10            1.10
 x.10           +.11
 .1100 =  .11 interest   1.21  amount at end of year 2
```

Year 3

```
$1.21            1.21
 x.10           +.12
 .1210 =  .12 interest   1.33  amount at end of year 3
```

Year 4

```
$1.33            1.33
 x.10           +.13
 .1330 =  .13 interest   1.46  amount at end of year 4
```

For Mathematicians Only

Year 5

$1.46
 x.10
.1460 = .14 interest

1.46
+.14
1.60 amount at end of year 5

Year 6

$1.60
 x.10
.1600 = .16 interest

1.60
+.16
1.76 amount at end of year 6

Year 7

$1.76
 x.10
.1760 = .17 interest

1.76
+.17
1.93 amount at end of year 7

Year 8

$1.93
 x.10
.1930 = .19 interest

1.93
+.19
2.12 amount at end of year 8

Year 9

$2.12
 x.10
.2120 = .21 interest

2.12
+.21
2.33 amount at end of year 9

Year 10

$2.33
 x.10
.2330 = .23 interest

2.33
+.23
2.56 amount at end of year 10

Year 11

$2.56
 x.10
.2560 = .25 interest

2.56
+.25
2.81 amount at end of year 11

For Mathematicians Only

Total Amount

Year 1 = 1.10
Year 2 = 2.21
Year 3 = 1.33
Year 4 = 1.46
Year 5 = 1.60
Year 6 = 1.76
Year 7 = 1.93
Year 8 = 2.12
Year 9 = 2.33
Year 10 = 2.56
Year 11 = 2.81
        ―――――
         20.21

All of this arithmetic means that a company earning $1.00 a share this year and expected to increase its earnings compounded at 10% a year over the next eleven years would earn $20.21 per share if each of its yearly earnings were added together.

If the stock is selling at a price of less than $20.21 (or $20 rounded off) a share, it would be considered undervalued and, therefore, attractive. If you were to translate this into a price earnings ratio, you would be buying an undervalued stock if it were selling at 20 times or less.

Using this method, a growth rate of 15% would return earnings of about $28.00, and carry a 28 or less price earnings ratio to be undervalued. On a 5% earnings rate, the total eleven years earnings would be about $14.90 and a price earnings ratio of 15 or less would make the stock attractive.

As you can see, the key to this method of compounding

For Mathematicians Only

earnings is to estimate the correct growth rate. The best way to do this is to figure out what its past growth rate has been and to assume that this will continue. Do not use some analyst's projection of the future.

One of the most widely circulated publications on Wall Street is Standard & Poor's "Earnings Forecaster." This has nothing in it except a list of earnings estimates made by leading brokerage and advisory firms. Do not rely on it. There are times when the earnings in it are way off. It is much safer to use the past and current earnings than to "crystal ball" them.

There are many ways to come up with the historic growth rate. One way is to plot the earnings on special graph paper that can be purchased from the National Association of Investment Clubs. This is a non-profit organization of investment clubs designed to help its members select stocks in a rational way. Part of its methodology is to plot, on special graph paper, the earnings per share over the past years of a company and to fix a line of growth that best approximates the growth rate.

APPLYING THE MATHEMATICS OF GROWTH

Probably the most conservative and easily handled method is the following one. We shall find *the average percent increase in earnings per share for four years.*

To show how this is done we will use one of the growth stocks we have already worked with: Allied Stores.

For Mathematicians Only

FIRST: put down the last five years earnings. (We need five in order to get the difference between the last four).

$$1974 = 4.40$$
$$1973 = 4.00$$
$$1972 = 3.08$$
$$1971 = 2.36$$
$$1970 = 1.72$$

SECOND: find the dollar and cents difference between each succeeding year.

$$1974 = 4.40 \quad + .40$$
$$1973 = 4.00 \quad + .92$$
$$1972 = 3.08 \quad + .72$$
$$1971 = 2.36 \quad + .64$$
$$1970 = 1.72$$

This is how the difference was figured:

$$1971 = 2.36$$
$$1970 = \underline{1.72} \text{ (Subtract)}$$
$$.64$$

THIRD: find the percentage of increase for each succeeding year.

$$1974 = 4.40 \quad + .40 = 10\%$$
$$1973 = 4.00 \quad + .92 = 30\%$$
$$1972 = 3.08 \quad + .72 = 30\%$$
$$1971 = 2.36 \quad + .64 = 37\%$$
$$1970 = 1.72$$

For Mathematicians Only

This is how the percentage difference was figured.

$$1971 = 2.36$$
$$1970 = \underline{1.72} \quad \text{(Subtract)}$$
$$.64$$

64 ÷ 172 = .37 = 37% growth from 1970 to 1971.

FOURTH: obtain the four year average earnings gain by adding all the gains together and dividing by 4.

Growth from 1973 to 1974 = 10%
Growth from 1972 to 1973 = 30%
Growth from 1971 to 1972 = 30%
Growth from 1970 to 1971 = 37%
$$\overline{107\%}$$

107% divided by 4 equals 26.7 or 27% for the average four year growth rate.

Here are the four steps again for finding the average 4 year growth rate:

1. Set down the earnings for the last 5 years.
2. Find the dollar and cents difference between each succeeding year.
3. Change each of these dollar and cents differences into percentages.
4. Obtain the four year average growth rate by adding all the gains together and dividing by 4.

Now that we have the all-important average growth rate figure, we will go back and use the compound interest method. Here's the problem:

For Mathematicians Only

Allied Stores, when the leading indicators gave a buy signal, earned $4.40 a share for its latest 12 month period and had an average 4 year growth rate of 27%. How much will its total earnings per share be at the end of 11 years? If these total earnings are equal to, or more than, the current price earnings ratio, the stock is a buy. The lower the P/E ratio when compared to the total earnings, the more undervalued the stock and, therefore, the better the buy.

A VALUABLE SHORT-CUT

It is not really necessary to work out the whole eleven years. Most of the time the totals of these growth companies will give very large figures after 11 years.

So it is only necessary to work the compounding until you hit a year at which the totals equal or exceed the current P/E ratio. The *smaller* the number of years it takes to do this the more of a bargain the stock is.

Now let's work out some examples. The first one is to answer our problem about Allied Stores. Was it undervalued? If it was, how undervalued was it?

The price of the stock at the end of May 1975, was 30-3/8, the latest 12 months earnings were $4.33, and the P/E ratio was 7.

The $4.33 is not necessarily the earnings for the fiscal year. They are for the last 4 quarters.

$30-3/8 divided by $4.33 (earnings gave us the P/E ratio of 7).

For Mathematicians Only

```
        YEAR 1                    YEAR 2
   4.33 (latest 12 mo. earn.)     5.50
   x.27 (ave. 4 yr. growth)       x.27
   ─────                          ─────
   1.17                           1.49

   4.33                           5.50
  +1.17                          +1.49
   ─────                          ─────
   5.50                           6.99
```

TOTALS
year 1 = 5.50
year 2 = 6.99   (add)
─────
12.49

There you have it. Allied Stores was very much a bargain. In only two years its total earnings exceeded its P/E ratio of 7.

Let's take another growth company we have already dealt with to see if it was undervalued. The company is Ametek. The price was 16-3/4, the latest 12 month's earnings were $2.31, and the P/E ratio was 7.

Here's the work-up in order to arrive at the average 4 year growth rate.

```
1974 = 2.21
              +.41 =  23%
1973 = 1.80
              +.52 =  40
1972 = 1.28
              +.36 =  39%
1971 =  .92
              +.16 =  21%
1970 =  .76
                     ─────
                     123% divided by 4 = 31%
```

Now we can start compounding.

For Mathematicians Only

```
      YEAR 1              YEAR 2
       2.31                3.03
       x.31                x.31
       ----                ----
        .72                 .94

       2.31                3.03
        .72 (add)           .94 (add)
       ----                ----
       3.03                3.97
```

              TOTALS
          year 1 = 3.03
          year 2 = 3.97 (add)

                   7.00

As you can see, Ametek was also a highly undervalued stock. In only two years its total earnings equalled its P/E ratio of 7.

Here is another example to help set this method in your memory. This time it's Borden, Inc. At the time the leading indicators gave a buy signal in May 1975, the price was 24-5/8, the latest 12 months earnings were $2.75 and the P/E ratio was 9.

Here's the trend of the earnings in order to figure out the average 4 year growth rate.

```
        1974 = 2.72
                    +.35 = 15%
        1973 = 2.37
                    +.19 =  9%
        1972 = 2.18
                    +.18 =  9%
        1971 = 2.00
                    +.17 =  9%
        1970 = 1.83
                           ----
                           42% divided by 4 = 11%
```

Now for the compounding:

For Mathematicians Only

```
     YEAR 1                    YEAR 2
     2.75                      3.05
     x.11                      x.11
     ----                      ----
      .30                       .34

     2.75                      3.05
      .30                       .34   (add)
     ----                      ----
     3.05                      3.39

     YEAR 3
     3.39
     x.11
     ----
      .37

     3.39
      .37  (add)
     ----
     3.76
                  TOTALS
             year 1 =  3.05
             year 2 =  3.39  (add)
                      -----
                       6.44
             year 3 =  3.76
                       6.44  (add)
                      -----
                      10.20
```

In the case of Borden, it took three years for its total earnings to exceed its P/E ratio of 9.

How about doing one more just to make sure you've got it. Olin Corp. has also been dealt with. When the indicators turned bullish, the price was 26-1/2, its latest 12 month's earnings were $4.45 and the P/E ratio was 5.

143

For Mathematicians Only

Here's the earnings for the last 4 years in order to calculate the average 4 year growth rate.

$$
\begin{aligned}
1974 &= 4.10 \\
1973 &= 2.25 \\
1972 &= 1.37 \\
1971 &= 1.24 \\
1970 &= 1.18
\end{aligned}
\quad
\begin{aligned}
+1.85 &= 82\% \\
+ .88 &= 64\% \\
+ .13 &= 10\% \\
+ .06 &= \underline{5\%} \\
& 161\% \text{ divided by } 4 = 40\%
\end{aligned}
$$

40% was some earnings growth!

TOTALS

YEAR 1

$$
\begin{array}{r}
4.45 \\
\times .40 \\ \hline
1.78
\end{array}
$$

$$
\begin{array}{r}
4.45 \\
1.78 \text{ (add)} \\ \hline
6.23
\end{array}
$$

In just one year Olin's total earnings exceeded its P/E ratio of 5! Now that was undervalued!

At this point, let's list these growth stock starting with the best buy. The best buy is the one that takes the least number of years for the total earnings to equal or exceed its P/E ratio.

For Mathematicians Only

Company	Years Needed
Olin Corp.	1
Allied Stores	2 (The total earn. exceeded the P/E of 7)
Ametek	2 (The total earn. equalled the P/E of 7)
Borden	3

Although all of these growth stocks were undervalued, the best buy was Olin Corp.

This may seem a lot of arithmetic, but it really isn't, especially if you have a pocket calculator. With one of these all you have to do is copy the numbers down ahead of time and then do all the figuring.

A SHORT-CUT OF A SHORT-CUT

Let's arrange the table differently:

Company	Average 4 Year Growth	Latest 12 Mos. P/E Ratio	Years Needed
Olin	40%	5	1
Allied Stores	27%	7	2
Ametek	31%	7	2
Borden	11%	9	3

1. For this short-cut all you do is divide the 4 year growth rate *into* the current P/E ratio. If this ratio, carried out to three decimal places, is higher than 1.000, leave the stock alone. If the ratio is lower than 1.000, it's undervalued. This is called the "price earnings gain multiple."

2. Put into rank order, the best buy first.

For Mathematicians Only

Now let's figure them out.

OLIN CORP
5 ÷ 40 = .125
ALLIED STORES
7 ÷ 27 = .259
AMETEK
7 ÷ 31 = .225
BORDEN
9 ÷ 11 = .817

Now we'll make a new chart incorporating this new ratio:

Company	Average 4 Year Growth	Latest 12 Mos. P/E Ratio	Years Needed	Price Earnings Gain Multiple
Olin	40%	5	1	.125
Allied Strs.	27%	7	2	.259
Ametek	31%	7	2	.225
Borden	11%	9	3	.817

Not one of these would have been eliminated because all of the ratios were under 1.000. Olin still shows up best on two counts:

1. It has the smallest number of years needed for its earnings to equal or exceed its P/E ratio;

2. It has the lowest "price earnings multiple."

This method is very fine and quite easy to use. It will

allow you to scan very quickly a large number of growth companies in a very short period of time. It sounds like a lot of work—but it really isn't.

CHAPTER 8

THE DEVIL THEORY—
Buy On Breaks, Sell On Rallies

THE DEVIL IN PAST TIMES

"The Devil made me do it," grins comedian Flip Wilson as he rationalizes some mischief he had just been up to. The audience bursts out in strident laughter, just as if they knew what the Devil was all about.

I'm sure that hardly any of them know anything about the concept, or else they would have frozen with horror. In fact, I think it's safe to say that the networks would never have allowed the expression to be used.

And for good reason! It's only been in the last 300 years or so that the mania of witch trials reached its peak in the notorious trials of 1692 in Salem, Massachusetts. Witches were supposed to have supernatural powers and were

The Devil Theory

servants of the Devil. They differed from sorcerers, wizards, warlocks and others who dealt in black magic in that these people were masters of the Devil. In order to be rid of a witch, one went for help to a wizard or a clergyman.

The idea of having a Devil is "the great out" when it comes to explaining away the miseries of mankind. In the Apocrypha of the Bible, demons or evil spirits are mentioned for the first time as the causes of calamities. The first mention of the Devil himself is in relation to the seduction of Eve. There, in the Apocryphal Wisdom of Solomon, it is said that through the Devil the necessity of death came into the world.

The New Testament contains distinct recognition of how popular it was to attribute the Devil to causing diseases. The names used are the Devil, Satan, the Adversary, the Old Serpent, the Great Dragon and Beelzebub.

The primitive Church considered the existence of the Devil to be an unquestionable fact. The majority of Christians held that all evil, physical as well as moral, was the work of the Devil and his demons.

If the fig trees did not produce, it was due to the Devil, rather than lack of water or fertilizer. If a wife could not conceive, it was the Devil's fault—not the malfunction of the male or female. If half the town's population died of the plague, it was not due to the rats but to the Devil. If a person believed in a somewhat different version of the Holy Text than his neighbors, then he had made a pact with the Devil.

Such a powerful, long standing concept seems to become part of the nervous system of the human race.

The Devil Theory

And even though the "civilized" world has underplayed it ever since the "Age of Enlightenment" and through our own "Atomic Age," every once in awhile the Devil manages to resurrect itself. This is especially true in troubled times when nothing that we do seems to work.

THE DEVIL IN MODERN GARB

And in difficult days we do live. Many of the same physical and moral evils that afflicted our earlier and simpler societies are confronting us now. Mini wars: not between Vandals and Goths or Italian Catholics and German Protestants, but between Irish Catholics and Protestants, and Middle East Mohammedans and Israeli Jews.

Disease: not between malaria and Bubonic Plague, but between Sickle Cell Anemia, Multiple Sclerosis and Schizophrenia.

Transportation: not between walking, or riding the horse, but between the car, or the plane, or the train, or the rocket.

Working Conditions: not with the peasants or the Medieval Guilds, but with the United Auto Workers or the American Federation of Teachers.

Capital and Trade: not with self-sufficient serfdoms but with international trade, balance-of-payments and imperialism.

Pollution: not with the proper placing of a water well, but with the water table of the whole continent, the air above and sea around.

The Devil Theory

You name it and we've got it—only more complex, and more difficult to solve. All of which leads some people backwards in time to search out and apply the "older solutions."

Some of the most popular television series are throwbacks to those times when the Devil was the cause. Picture them: "Bewitched," "Nanny and the Professor," "Ghost Story." Recall the books: "The Exorcist," "Possessed." "The Shape of Illusion," and "Rosemary's Baby."

THE DEVILS OF WALL STREET

This phenomena seems to be growing. Since operating profitably in the stock market is among the most difficult and frustrating of activities, you can be sure that there are a number of people who ascribe to the Devil as being the trouble-maker. Sometimes the Devil is alluded to vaguely as "they" or "the Syndicates" or "the Banks." Once in awhile, a finger is pointed at some specific group.

Richard Ney, in his "The Wall Street Jungle," has attacked the specialist as the latest Devil. The specialist is the market maker who stands at the trading post and tries to make a continuous and fair market in his stock. This means that the price differences between each transaction are to be small ones, like eighths and quarters, not halves and dollars.

Ney's vehemence proclaims that "there is more sheer lunacy per square foot on the floor of the New York Stock Exchange than any place else in the world." He goes on to say that in many situations specialists "have the power

The Devil Theory

to set and control prices unilaterally." According to him, it is this modern Devil, the exchange's specialists, that cause investors to get a raw deal.

Other "observers" point to alternate Devils. One of the best is the "anti-chartists." These are the groups, including the specialists, who lay waiting to ambush the chartists. (A chartist is a believer that stock prices can be predicted solely by the internal workings of the market itself—its price movements and its volume characteristics).

No matter which technical system a chartist uses, whether it be point and figure, bar charts, moving averages, tick volume, on-balance-volume, relative strength, or what have you, each has to know when a stock has broken out or broken down, when each movement is a continuation or a reversal.

By whatever definition he uses, the chartist will buy on a break-out, hoping for higher prices, and sell on break-downs. This may sound fairly cut-and-dried, but it isn't. What used to work on the charts for years hasn't done so well in recent times. The price of a stock no sooner rallies above a congestion area for a chart breakout, than it attracts a wad of selling that kills the move. A price will no sooner break down under a previous dip or a trend-line, catching stops, than large buying comes in. Result: one whip-saw after another; one loss after another.

In fact, this has happened so often that a whole new school of thought has come into being—the "random walkers." These are the professors who have plugged all kinds of data into their computers and because they haven't been able to figure any predictable patterns, have

The Devil Theory

thrown up their hands in frustration and have written many impressive papers, all of which say there is no way to pick them but the pin system. They contend that stock prices do not move in any predictable patterns, only in random ways. What went up a minute ago can just as likely come down the following minute. What went up last week could just as well retreat this week.

Forget your waves and cycles and patterns. Just buy and hold. It'll all work out in the long run. Don't take my word for it. Read Paul Cootner's "The Random Character of Stock Market Prices."

So here is the latest Devil, "The Anti-Chartists," all dressed up in the modern garb of computers and statistics and university authority.

But, even if what they say is true, there is no cause for alarm. Of course trends are broken, patterns are reversed and chartists are whipsawed. But there are no Devils. The reasons are rational: war breaks out, a president is assassinated, the balance-of-payments gets out of whack, a major strike occurs, government passes legislation—there are a lot of good "non-devil" reasons.

HOW TO TAKE ADVANTAGE OF THE DEVIL

We are going to take advantage of these temporary shake-outs to buy on breaks and sell on rallies. To counter those who wish to attribute these break-downs to evil forces, I am going to develop the "Devil Theory of Trading."

Before we begin, we must have faith in one overarching

The Devil Theory

principal: that earnings will in time determine the price of the stock. As long as the previous four years' earnings are up, and of the last four quarters, each succeeding quarter is higher, the price of the stock must eventually rise. Along the way there may be some price reversals, but like a good general, our strategy will take advantage of them.

Let's go over the technical method again.

1. Plot only weekly closes.

2. A "buy" signal occurs when prices go up, then down, and then go up again, this time getting above the previous peak by at least 2 points (Under a price level of 10, use only 1 point).

3. A sell signal occurs when prices thrust down below the highest close by at least 20%.

It was pointed out that the reasons for buying on break-outs instead of reactions were two:

1. If prices have broken down they may have done so for good reasons: a poor earnings report is about to be reported, a law suit is going to hit the company (like Westinghouse), a strike is about to take place, or any number of rational causes.

2. The breaking down may be due to the deterioration of the stock market in general. That is, without our realization, the market has slipped to the bearish side. Under those circumstances we wouldn't want to be long anyway.

However, as long as the leading indicators continue upward most of the reactions of growth stocks are irrational. These shake-outs may be taken advantage of by using the "Devil Theory."

The Devil Theory is almost the reversal of our usual method as repeated above. To implement it, we simply do

The Devil Theory

the opposite of what we usually do.

All you do is wait for a dip off of any high of at least 7% or more. (Obviously, if the slide continues to our 20% mark we will have to sell out). Then buy on the very next up-turn. Sell out when the stock makes new highs. (If a stock is bullish it's supposed to go up in some sort of step pattern with each step, of course, becoming that new high). Now don't get impatient—you'll see what I mean in a minute.

Turn to the chart on Allied Stores, Figure 4 on page 63. The dip from "3" to "c" = 40-1/2 to 35 = 13%. That's enough of a dip. The turn-up came a week after "C" at 35-1/2. Sell at the new high at 42.

The dip from "D" to "a" = 46-1/2 to 43 = 7-1/2%. That's enough of a dip. The turn-up and buy came a week after "a" at 43-1/2. Sell at the new high of 48.

Turn to the chart on Ametek, Figure 5 on page 68. The dip from "2" to "3" = 19-1/8 to 15-5/8 = 18%. That's plenty. The turn-up came a week after "3" at 16-3/4. Buy. Sell at the high of 24-1/8. (The new high before this was 19-1/2—not enough of a profit).

The dip from "a" to "6" = 24-3/8 to 19-7/8 = 18%. The turn-up and buy came the week after "6" at 20-3/4. Sell at the new high at "b" at 24-3/4.

Turn to the chart on Bendix, Figure 6 on page 73. The dip from "B" to "a" = 43 to 39-1/4 = 9%. The turn-up and buy came a week after "a" at 39. Sell at the new high of 43-3/4. (There were other signals, but I'll let you figure these out).

One last time. Turn to Borden, Figure 7 on page 78. The dip from "a" to "b" = 25-1/8 to 23 = 8%. The turn-up

The Devil Theory

and buy came the week after "b" at 24. Sell at the new high of 27-1/2.

And there you have the "Devil Theory" for buying on breaks and selling on rallies. As you can see, this is a trading technique. It will not produce long term capital gains—only profits.

CHAPTER 9

TURNING DISASTERS INTO PROFITS—
Or Buying The Industry Group With The Most Potential

If you can make money by going long in a bear market, then it should be a cinch to do so in a bull market. You can succeed in a bear market by turning disasters into profits, as shown in this chapter.

It seems that every year, whether the economy is booming or busting, our society has such a need for certain products and services that those companies which supply those products must garner large profits, thus raising the prices of their stocks.

I will cover the four bear markets of the last decade. Although the "Sizzling Sixties" had its share of bull markets, there were five significant sell-offs: 1960, 1962, 1966,1969, and 1973-4.

Turning Disasters Into Profits

THE BEAR MARKET OF 1960 AND PROFITS

To refresh your memory, let me sketch in some background for 1960. This was the beginning, as stock market pundits put it, of the "Sizzling Sixties." The newly elected President was John Kennedy, having beaten Richard Nixon in a very close race. This was the first time that two presidential candidates debated on television. President Kennedy's political thesis was summed up in his "The New Frontier." This led to one off-shoot, the "Peace Corps," where young Americans could apply their energy, enthusiasm and altruism in the doing of good works.

Some of the important movies of 1960 were: "Elmer Gantry," a study of a con man in religion; "Sunrise at Campobello," an in-depth study of a crucial slice out of the life of F.D.R.; and "Psycho," a Hitchcockian thriller that for a time took the joy out of having a shower.

A few memorable books were "Advise and Consent," describing the zig-zag workings of the U.S. Senate; "Hawaii," a gargantuan historical novel that was to be made into two movies; and "How I Made Two Million Dollars in the Stock Market," by economist and ballroom dancer Nicolas Darvis, who actually made it and subsequently lost most of it, but whose phenomenal financial climb gave rise to a whole new generation of market players.

The economic and stock market picture of 1960 shows that both were suffering from financial anemia. Corporate profits were lower. To stimulate buying power for securities, margins were reduced from 90% to 70%. But

Turning Disasters Into Profits

the country wasn't going to the dogs. For the first time in our history, 70 million people had jobs, even though unemployment rose to 5%. This dichotomy was blamed on the slow rate of economic growth and the increasing use of automation. (You will soon see that one of the largest bull moves in the 1960 bear market was by the companies which dealt in automation).

Further retarding growth was Congress, which refused to cut taxes. Consequently, we saw the market top out at 685 on the Dow in January, and, by the following October, fall 15% to 566. High volume—5 million shares—occurred just twice that year. Government bonds yielded 4-1/2%. A steel strike had taken place, and tight money prevailed because inventories had to be rebuilt.

Here we have the typical causes for the bear market slide of 15%. Yet two stock groups defied the inertial down movement: the savings and loans, which went up 70%, and the vending machines—the automata—which scored a 71% gain. What were the disasters that produced such huge gains for these two industries?

Let us explore the savings and loan group first. We will shift to Los Angeles County, California. From 1950 to 1960 there was a massive population growth requiring an equally explosive build-up of housing. Sitting right in the middle of this was the largest concentration of savings and loan companies in the country willing and able to supply the mortgage money.

The magnets that drew this influx of population were the electronics and defense industries which discovered that Hollywood wasn't unique in realizing the benefits of sunshine and ideal weather. It was rather easy to convert

Turning Disasters Into Profits

the orange groves and small ranches that composed most of Los Angeles county to residential housing. By 1960 there were 6 million people being serviced by 90 savings and loans and 100 of their branches. Their assets grew from 950 million dollars to 6 billion. Savings accounts increased from 750 million to 4 billion, resulting in 40% of the homes being financed by them. There was only one way for these savings and loan stocks to go—and that was up!

Some of the companies that haven't been absorbed and are still traded on the New York Stock Exchange are: Financial Federation, which went from 14 to 32, more than doubling itself, and a year later soared to 91; First Charter Financial, which doubled from 10 to 20, and hit 50 before 1961 was over; and Great Western Financial, which started at 10 and started the new year with a price tag of 19, finally topping 46 the following year.

The second disaster of 1960 also grew out of population growth. This was the build-up in the labor force which necessitated more efficient ways for mass feeding. Ready to benefit were the vending machines and their helpmates, the coin-changers. These machines started to sell everything from peanuts to panties; from dinners to digestion pills.

This was the statistical background: up until this time, 300,000 workers were needed just to mass feed 24 million of their fellows; labor costs were at the high point where some of the food vender operations were losing money, and the constant increase of labor needed more in-plant feeding. Even though large numbers of workers were being fed, 96% of all the factories had no hot food or full

Turning Disasters Into Profits

line vending facilities. Here was a tremendous potential!

The food machines took over—shades of Charlie Chaplin's "Modern Times." These gave birth to their mechanical brothers, the coin-changers. Paper money had to be exchanged for coins. By 1960 there were 4 million of these silent salesmen with sales topping 2 billion dollars.

Two of the companies still around are U.M.C., whose stock sky-rocketed from 28 to 70, and Vendo Corporation, whose price started at 19 and hit 51, both during the bear market of 1960.

THE BEAR MARKET OF 1962 AND PROFITS

The next bear market was 1962. Mr. Kennedy was still President and engaged in some political fence mending in the Mid-West when he suddenly had to hurry back to Washington. We were told that he had developed a head cold. It turned out that the Russians had provided the virus in the form of the Cuban missile crisis. This is the time that the civil rights movement went into full swing, with James Meredith being the first black to be enrolled at Mississippi University. Outerspace efforts, spurred on by the Russians, finally bore fruit with John Glenn becoming the first American to orbit the earth.

To refresh your memories of 1962, here are some of the most memorable movies. "Cleopatra" and "Mutiny on the Bounty," the former full of the pageantry of ancient Egypt and the latter of the South Seas, were both financial busts. "The Greatest Story Every Told" featured Christ as the revolving theme, whereas "Lawrence of Arabia"

Turning Disasters Into Profits

centered on a demi-god. And one of the first erotic sex films, "Lolita," pandered to our suppressed puritan natures.

The best sellers of 1962 were "Ship of Fools," subsequently made into a movie; "Life in Court," by the famous lawyer, Louis Nizer; "The Rothchilds," recently converted to a musical; "Silent Spring," which gave added impetus to the new puritans, the ecological movement; and "Sex and the Single Girl," another excursion into erotica.

1962 has been dubbed the "Kennedy Bear Market" for good reasons. When the steel companies decided to raise prices to offset increasing costs, the President had an "eyeball to eyeball" confrontation with them, going so far as to threaten to cut off all government steel purchases from any company that wouldn't cooperate. Zing! This led to the sharpest market decline in 25 years. From an all time high in December of 1961 of 726 on the Dow, the market depth charged to a low of 535 in June of 1962. This was a 30% drop which saw 150 billion dollars in paper profits disappear. At least the President stopped, however temporarily, the wage-price spiral.

Since the market was so depressed, margins were cut from the 70% level of the 1960 bear market to 50%, in an attempt to provide buying support. On May 28th, known as Black Tuesday in market history, prices dropped a whopping 6-1/2% and volume soared to almost 15 million shares. This classic textbook example of a selling climax was triggered by the Cuban missile crisis. (It should be pointed out that the mutual funds behaved as unsophisticated as the public. Instead of buying securities when they

Turning Disasters Into Profits

were being dumped, fund purchases dried up).

Nevertheless, there were two industries that bucked the tide; the airlines and the sugar industry. What social disaster was imminent so that the airlines would benefit?

Business was growing rapidly, thrusting out more complex tentacles over larger geographical areas. No longer was it necessary to direct corporate matters via the train or auto. Now an executive could be vacationing in Miami, receive a hurry-up phone call, jet back to New York in a couple of hours, make his decisions and return to Miami almost before his martini got warm. The new comfortable jets had finally come into their own.

But who would have guessed it? The statistics up until this time showed the airlines to be in sad financial shape. Floyd Hall, president of Eastern, said, "We used to be too enthralled with the helmet and goggle era. We used to stand around and cheer for 15 minutes every time a plane took off!" That's how slow business was. There was such excessive competition that Northeast Airlines had passed the point of no return. There were just too many seat-miles to fill. The high cost of changing from pistons to jets and the mounting interest payments on the debt was tremendous. In 1961, the trunk lines lost 30 million dollars and profits hit an 11 year low.

Apparently, it is always darkest before dawn: the 1962 statistics suddenly showed light. Passenger service increased 14% and air cargo picked up 25%. The competing cars and trains just couldn't whisk businessmen, vacationers and servicemen to their destinations as quickly as these speedy jets. So the airlines came out of their tailspins into great flying weather.

Turning Disasters Into Profits

American Airlines that year went from 7-1/2 to 12, Delta moved from 1-1/2 to 5-1/2 and Eastern from 8 to 14. The momentum continued for 5 more years when American peaked at 47, Delta topped at 44 (after being split) and Eastern soared to 60.

The next group to thumb its nose at the "Kennedy Bear Market" were the sugars. There is an important lesson to be learned here. Since sugar is a commodity and is traded on a spot and futures basis, it is very important to see whether those futures are bearish or bullish. Almost invariably, when the commodity that a company's profits depends upon turns bullish, then the profits of that company will also increase. (An exception is the meat packing companies. When cattle futures or pork bellies take a nose dive, the raw material of the packers becomes cheaper and, therefore, their profits rise).

But sugar is the norm and in 1962 sugar futures burst all bounds of upside reason. Sugar futures soared from under 2 cents a pound to over 11 cents a pound. At $11.20 for each one-hundredth of a cent move, or $1120 for each penny increase in a pound of sugar, such a gigantic bull move netted the fortunate speculator, who had bought for 2 cents and sold for 11 cents, a grand profit of $11,080. Since he had put down an initial margin of not more than $500.00 per contract, the percentage gain was a fantastic 2200%. (Although this was theoretically possible, I don't personally know of anyone who was so lucky or skilled to make that kind of killing).

What confluence of events occurred for such a wild move? Up until 1962, low sugar prices had forced marginal producers out and the world ended up with less

Turning Disasters Into Profits

and less production. Weather in eastern Europe, where sugar beets are harvested, turned unfavorable so that beet production had decreased. Then Castro took over Cuba and not only impaired sugar production, but what was left had to be used to pay the Russians for their help. Finally, in order to make up for the loss of Cuban sugar imports, Congress passed new legislation for current U.S. sugar beet and sugar cane producers (and 12 other countries) to supply half of what Cuba's quota had been.

How much sweeter could an investment be? Two companies still around reaped handsome profits. American Sugar moved from 14-1/2 to 21-1/2 that year, and the following year saw it at 30-1/2. Sucrest almost doubled in those two years going from 10-1/2 to 19.

THE BEAR MARKET OF 1966 AND PROFITS

The next bear market we encounter is that of 1966. Lyndon B. Johnson is President. Having inherited the Vietnam War from his assassinated predecessor, and attempting to maintain the continuity of government after such a major tragedy by implementing and expanding those on-going policies, Mr. Johnson enlarged the war while simultaneously pushing through legislation for civil rights and the poor. His was a government of "guns and butter."

France, under the rule of De Gaulle, quit NATO. Johnson dispatched troops to quell an insurrection in the Dominican Republic. Since the health of the President is uppermost to his people, Mr. Johnson forwarded the most

Turning Disasters Into Profits

detailed account of his operation, complete with pictures, that the American public had ever been privy to. 1966 saw the rise of Stokely Carmichael and Black Power. James Meredith was murderously shot while walking through Mississippi. The Supreme Court extended the rights of man through the famous law decision called "The Miranda Case."

Some of the talked about movies of 1966 were "Who's Afraid of Virginia Wolf," a tale of the strange symbiosis of a husband and adventurous wife; "Thunderball," modern man's new hero worship of the sex-adventurer; "Hawaii," based on the Michener book of 1960; and "A Man for All Seasons," providing us with historical insight.

Books that were widely read included two that challenged the establishment. Ralph Nader's "Unsafe at Any Speed," harpooned the auto industry. "How to Avoid Probate," was a do-it-yourself manual on how to keep lawyers and the courts from milking your estate. The aftermath of the Kennedy Tragedy turned up in two best sellers, "Death of a President" by William Manchester and the "Warren Report" on the Kennedy Assassination. Then there were two books dealing with psychological aberrations, "Valley of the Dolls" and "In Cold Blood."

The market at this time was feeling its "cheerioats." On February 9th, it punched through the magic 1000 on the Dow, hitting an intra-day high of 1001.01 and closed at 995.15. But that proved to be the all-time high, for by October the Dow plunged 25% to 744. (This was the second time a bear market low was made in October).

A paradox had developed; this was the sixth year of a

Turning Disasters Into Profits

booming economy—witness higher car sales for one statistic—and yet the market was retreating. Was it signaling a recession? Inflation was uppermost. Johnson expressed concern that his 3.2% guidelines were being breached, but he didn't do anything. The last straw was in September when Congress refused to extend the 7% investment tax credit and accelerated the depreciation rate. Tight money, higher interest rates and increased government spending on Vietnam were the causes of the market slide. You just couldn't support both "guns and butter."

Even with the market plunging 25%, we find one industry charging upwards for a 66% gain. That was a new exotic metal called beryllium. What was the disaster here that allowed investors to make handsome profits?

The new powerful jets needed a super metal for rudders, brake discs and navigation instruments. Also, NASA, having just put John Glenn into orbit, was rapidly coming on with the need for sophisticated, miniaturized electronic instruments. Concurrently, the Atomic Energy Commission was building peace-time reactors to produce electricity. Here we have a solution sitting in our laps; a metal stronger than steel, lighter than aluminum, able to withstand great heat—the new space-age metal, beryllium. Furthermore, it was found that the addition of a pinch of beryllium to copper produced a wire of steel-like strength and high electric conductivity, ideal for electronic computers and miniaturized instruments.

Brush Beryllium, the largest producer, trading over-the-counter, moved from 10 to 20 and one year later peaked at 42-5/8.

Turning Disasters Into Profits

Another industry that bucked the market by rising 62% was air freight. The disaster affecting us was obvious. The Vietnam War was expanding considerably and war logistics called for more and more supplies. Foreign trade was increasing. Containerization, the latest innovation for distribution, had come into its own, even forcing Europe to get on the bandwagon. The airline companies were already prepared by specializing in large capacity jet freighters. Cargo tonnage increased 40%.

In 1966, Emery Air Freight went from 28-1/2 to 48-1/4, Flying Tiger from 12 to 25-1/2, and Seaboard World Airlines from 13-3/4 to 30.

THE BEAR MARKET OF 1969 AND PROFITS

1969—What a way to end the "Sizzling Sixties!" We started with the bear market in 1960 and ended with one in 1969. It seems the only way you could have survived those ten years was by taking speedy Alka-Seltzer. This last bear market was the year that was: the worst since the crash of 1929.

Nevertheless, one group soared nearly 60%—the pollution industry. Those wise enough to spot it cleaned up on cleanup.

From ignominious defeat in the Governor's race for California when he said to reporters, "you won't have Richard Nixon to kick around anymore," to the loss by a hair of the presidential election to John Kennedy, and finally to his victory over Hubert Humphrey, Richard Nixon was finally acting out his greatest dream—that of

Turning Disasters Into Profits

being President. Calling his program "The New Federalism," he tried to limit the power of the Federal Government.

Among the massive problems he faced, two were uppermost: the solution of the Vietnam War and the runaway inflation caused by Johnson's "guns and butter" program. The war worsened and so did inflation. The cost of military equipment for the war and NATO made money short for domestic programs. It was his effort to curb inflation that put the kiss of death on the lips of the already ailing market.

Tight money, illiquidity of many corporations, margin calls and the selling these induced, soaring interest rates, and broker's bankruptcies filled even the strongest stomachs with the acid feelings of 1929.

To make matters worse, there was a concerted outrage and outcry against pollution of all kinds.

On October 3, 1969, a plane carrying Dr. Roger Egeberg, the assistant Secretary of Health, Education and Welfare, flew from Washington to Detroit. The plane circled over Detroit for an hour and a half. The pilot still couldn't get through the smoke and fog and had to return to Washington. Dr. Egeberg was supposed to give a speech at a conference sponsored by the National Federation of Business and Professional Women's Clubs. The conference was on clean air.

The irony of this news clipping is that this incident was wide spread. The "gag"—and I mean this in both the facetious and literal sense—was on us.

A group of angry citizens in Pittsburgh sued U.S. Steel for millions of dollars because the air pollution was

Turning Disasters Into Profits

ruining their neighborhoods.

Professor Julius Goldberg found that highly polluted areas of Chicago had significantly higher death rates than areas of lower pollution. Goldberg collected figures from 20 stations around the country as an additional part of his work. His statistics showed that for people of moderate incomes who had died from pneumonia, there were 95 deaths for every 100,000 in high pollution areas as against about half that rate—or 46—in low pollution areas.

One day, the Philadelphia Gas Works had a "shocker" of an ad in the papers. There was a half page picture of a body laid out in a coffin surrounded by beautiful flowers. The caption was: "Here lies Robert Elliott. He breathed to death." The blurb underneath ended with: "Write your Congressman; your mayor; tell your committeeman; talk to your neighbors; *SCREAM!*"

Just as bad as air pollution is, all you had to do was look at the ground to see all the water pollution. Lake Erie, the Schuylkill and Delaware Rivers had all turned into running sewers. Fish couldn't live and people couldn't fish: Industry's need for clean, cheap water, as well as our thirst for a glass of "de-chemicalized" water, could not be satisfied.

In fact, the House Appropriations Committee voted more than double the funds President Nixon had requested for water pollution. Despite this boost, Representative Dingell of Michigan said $600 million wasn't enough. He sputtered, "We want a $1 billion appropriation and that's what we intend to press for..."

The accumulation of solid wastes reached alarming proportions. Each person threw away twice as much as he

Turning Disasters Into Profits

did fifty years ago. And every year, we increased our throwaways by two percent. This, added to the two percent annual population growth, increased the amount of solid wastes by 4%. The wealthier we became, the bigger the problem. Our riches began to bury us.

The companies that attacked, and helped to solve, this "grave" problem made a lot of money. The price of their stocks mushroomed. American Air Filter moved from a low of 25 to a 1969 high of 65, an appreciation of 160%. Research-Cottrell whisked from 32 to 68, a rise of 112%. Zurn Industries ran from 21 to 38, a price increase of 80%. Joy Manufacturing took off from 26 and peaked out at 53, for a heady profit of 103%.

ILLUSTRATIONS FROM THE 1970 BEAR MARKET AND THE ENSUING BULL MARKET

In January of 1971, when our leading indicators gave the signal for a bull market, was there a societal crisis so that we could have profited if we had bought the right companies in the proper industry? There sure was—the energy industry. Natural gas and oil were in short supply.

In 1970, according to the American Gas Association, gas production had increased about 1 trillion cubic feet to 21.8 trillion cubic feet. But additions to U.S. reserves within the continental U.S. came to only 11.5 trillion, causing total reserves to fall to about 256 trillion cubic feet. This meant only a 12 year supply at the 1970 rate of consumption. The importance of increasing natural gas reserves was underlined when the Federal Power Com-

Turning Disasters Into Profits

mission granted higher prices to gas producers.

Not only do we search for the best growth companies supplying oil and gas, but also for those allied to the industry, those supplying oil well machinery and services.

Here are the figures on the four companies in the oil and gas industry that met the fundamentals for growth situations. For each of the previous 4 years their earnings were higher, and each of their latest four quarter earnings were up

MOBIL OIL

Years

1970 = 4.77
1969 = 4.50
1968 = 4.26
1967 = 3.80
1966 = 3.51

Quarters

	1970	1969
March	1.16	1.13
June	1.09	1.04
September	1.19	1.10
December	1.33	1.23

The price at the end of January, 1971, was 52-1/2. Between this time and the end of the year, Mobil Oil had hit a high of 60.

Turning Disasters Into Profits

SABINE ROYALTY (on AMEX)

Years

1970 = .92
1969 = .79
1968 = .70
1967 = .64
1966 = .52

Quarters

	1970	1969
March	.22	.21
June	.19	.17
September	.21	.19
December	.26	.19

The price at the end of January, 1971, was 19-1/2. Between this time and the end of 1971, Sabine Royalty hit a high of 29.

SCHLUMBERGER LIMITED

Years

1970 = 4.23
1969 = 3.99
1968 = 3.54
1967 = 2.76
1966 = 2.46

Turning Disasters Into Profits

Quarters

	1970	1969
March	.93	.90
June	1.02	.93
September	1.05	1.02
December	1.23	1.14

The price at the end of January, 1971, was 95. By the end of 1971, Schlumberger had hit a high of 156.

TEXAS OIL & GAS

1970 = 1.96
1969 = 1.56
1968 = 1.28
1967 = 1.16
1966 = 1.00

Quarters

	1970	1969
November	.36	.28
February	.44	.36
May	.52	.40
August	.64	.52

The price at the end of January, 1971, was 28. By the end of 1971, Texas Oil & Gas had hit a high of 51-1½.

AN ILLUSTRATION FROM THE 1973-4 BEAR MARKET

Turning Disasters Into Profits

The bear markets of 1973-4 again demonstrated that you could have bucked the down move by buying a growth stock in the sugar industry. As you can see from the previous example given for 1962, sugar periodically leads to major profits. The last time was back when Castro seized Cuba. What happened this time?

Prices went sky-high for three particular reasons. The first was that Mother Nature, that old fertility deity, decided to go to the Land-of-No-Return. A drought occurred that caused considerable damage to the crop.

Secondly, Congress failed to pass the Sugar Act. What effect did this have? While the Sugar Act was on the books, we were guaranteed an ample supply of sugar. Those countries that supplied us with sugar were provided a market and we gave them guarantees to pay them enough so that they would make a profit. But when the Act died, free competition set in.

But the competition couldn't have come at a worse time. The world drought gave those overseas producers a bonanza. They could now sell their sugar for whatever the market would bear and to whomever they pleased. (Remember the prices of soft drinks going up and people stealing sugar from restaurants?)

As the stockpile of sugar dwindled and the punishing drought continued, other countries felt the pinch as we did. This is the third reason sugar prices bolted up: Great Britain, Egypt, and others with a sweet tooth came barreling into the market jamming prices higher.

Out of the three major companies in the sugar industry, only one was a growth company—Holly Sugar.

Turning Disasters Into Profits

Here were the four year earnings:

> 1973 = 3.41
> 1972 = 1.70
> 1971 = 1.41
> 1970 = .72
> 1969 = deficit of 1.59

(Just because there was a deficit in 1969 does not throw a monkey wrench in our method for determining growth companies. Notice that we do have 4 years of higher growth. Isn't 1970's earnings better than 1969's? Of course they are. And so on up the line).

Holly Sugar does not report its earnings until the end of its third quarter. Although this is highly unusual, it does make sense for this company because it gives it time to reasonably determine its major costs. In this case only the last two quarters were considered and they were higher.

	1973-4	1972-3
9 mos. Dec.	2.21	1.35
12 mos. March	1.20	.35
	3.41	1.70

The price of Holly was 12 at the middle of 1973. By the middle of 1975 the price was 32. By the middle of 1976, the price hit a high of over 46!

Throughout bear markets, certain industries forge ahead. It is a wonder to behold when you see a handful of stocks first lifting their heads and then their bodies out of the collapsing debris of the rest of the stock list. The

Turning Disasters Into Profits

answer, of course, is that these companies are profiting by solving the needs of society.

By latching on to them you, too, can turn disasters into profits.

CHAPTER 10

LET THE YELLOW PAGES DO YOUR WALKING—

Or How To Pick The Strongest Stocks

The relative strength concept is very much like a horse race. As the race for investment profits continues, certain stocks gain momentum and lead the pack while others start slipping back. By the end of the course, the winners easily stand out.

WHAT RELATIVE STRENGTH IS

Relative strength deals with the *Trend* of a stock's price relative to some standard or base. It owes its value to the observed fact that security prices, more often than not, will act like Sir Isaac Newton's second law of motion. Stock prices usually show a persistency of trend.

Let's consider two stocks. Stock "A" over a period of

Let The Yellow Pages Do Your Walking

time slips from 100 to 90 while stock "B" sells down from 50 to 40. Both have lost 10 points. However, *On Relative Strength Basis*, stock "A" is acting better than stock "B." How do we know? A little arithmetic will show that stock "A" was down only 10%, whereas stock "B" was down 20%.

If, during the same time, the general market had been down 15%, the first stock would have appeared to be strong.

These relative trends more often than not maintain their momentum. Our problem is to determine the strongest stocks.

THE TOOLS YOU'LL NEED—
AND HOW TO USE THEM

The tools that are needed are simple enough. Just buy Barron's or save the Saturday or Sunday newspapers. That way you can get the weekly closes whenever you need them. And of course a pocket calculator would be very handy.

Now let's apply the relative strength concept to some growth stocks. Our basing point from which to start the comparison will be the closing price at the end of the previous year. In this case it will be 1974. What we are trying to do is to see which of our growth stocks had acted the strongest at the time the market turned up.

Let The Yellow Pages Do Your Walking

Stock	Price End 1974	Price As of 5/26/75	% Up	Rank Order	High of 1976	% Up	Rank Order
Abbott Labs (2/1 split)	25	34-3/4	39	4	55-1/4	59	3
Albertson's	12-7/8	18	40	3	23-7/8	33	6
Am. Nat. Gas	35-3/8	35-5/8	0	7	44-5/8	25	7
Ander. Clayton (2/1 split)	10-5/8	14-1/8	33	5	25	77	2
Bearings	13-1/2	22-1/2	67	2	31-3/4	41	5
Big Three (2/1 split)	22-3/4	26-1/2	16	6	40-1/2	53	4
Blue Bell (2/1 split)	6-1/8	13-7/8	127	1	29-3/8	112	1

These seven stocks, which were taken from the chapter on "Buying Grade 'A' Companies," shows that more often than not a good relative strength reading tends to produce better than average results. As you can see from the chart, the poorest in relative strength at the turn of the market was Am. Nat. Gas. It also underperformed the rest of the list, although it did advance 25%. Blue Bell was the best. Starting out at the gate with a relative strength of 127%, it just kept going all the way for a gain of 112% more.

Suppose we look at some of the stocks we've already worked with. Here's the chart.

183

Let The Yellow Pages Do Your Walking

Stock	Price End 1974	Price As of 5/26/75	% Up	Rank Order	High of 1976	% Up	Rank Order
Borden	19-3/4	24-5/8	25	6	34	38	6
Ametek	10-3/8	16-3/4	61	3	29-1/2	77	3
Bendix (4/3 split)	16	25-3/8	59	4	46-1/2	83	2
Olin Corp.	14-3/4	26-1/2	80	1	45-1/8	70	4
Super Value (2/1 split)	6-7/8	11-1/4	64	2	24-1/2	118	1
Universal Leaf (2/1 split)	12-5/8	19-1/8	51	5	31-1/4	63	5

Once again most of these stocks maintained the same pace they had at the start of the race. The worst performer was Borden, and that's how she ended up. Nevertheless, the stock did increase 38%. That's the value of buying a growth stock in the first place. The best performer was Super Value. She certainly lived up to her name by increasing a whopping 118%.

By using relative strength in conjunction with the growth stocks you can let those yellow S and P tear sheets do your walking for you.

CHAPTER 11

HOW TO BUY "GRADE A" GROWTH COMPANIES—
And Milk Them For Profits

The Philadelphia sports fans that attended the games of their home-town's professional teams were thoroughly disgusted in the early 1970's. Sitting at the bottom of the pile were the Phillies—the baseball team, the Philadelphia Eagles—the football team, and the 76ers—the basketball team.

At no time within memory have the pros of a major city done so little for so many. The spectators displayed their frustrations with booing, catcalls, the hanging of bed sheets with "Tose must go," and the tossing of beer cans (which had to be replaced by paper cups).

Things were so bad that even the bookies were reluctant to take bets.

Len Tose, owner of the beleaguered Eagles, fired his coach and staff after the '72 season. He was looking for a

How To Buy "Grade A" Growth Companies

head coach that was quality personified. After many months of searching, he picked Mike McCormack.

Mike was one of the staff which had turned the losing Washington Redskins into a title contender. In horse racing terms, Mike was by Paul Brown out of Vince Lombardi by George Allen. That was some "blood line." That was quality!

That's what this chapter is all about—quality. Would you rather eat a steak or a stew? How about driving a Cadillac instead of a Volks? Or Alpo for your dog instead of cereals? What about wearing a GGG suit as against a Robert Hall? Or the New York Times versus the Atlantic City Press. Compare Gypsy Rose Lee with the local stripper, Billy Dioux. In each instance the quality would be chosen.

WHAT IS MEANT BY QUALITY GROWTH STOCKS

There is a way, fortunately quite an easy one, for us to start our initial screening of growth companies for those that are "grade A" quality. By letting the Standard & Poor's rating system help us, we can get off to a running start.

Standard & Poor's, in their monthly stock summary book, explains their rating system:

A+	= Highest	B+	= Average
A	= High	B	= Below Average
A-	= Above Average	B-	= Low
		C	= Lowest

How To Buy "Grade A" Growth Companies

They say that the "relative quality" of common stocks cannot be measured, as can that of bonds, since it depends upon the degree of protection for interest and principal. However, there are differences in the nature of stocks, and some of them are well worth measuring and comparing.

Standard & Poor's rankings are designed to indicate by the use of symbols the relative stability and growth of earnings, and the relative stability and growth of dividends. These measures of past records have a considerable bearing on relative quality, but do not pretend to reflect an examination of all other factors, tangible and intangible, that also bear on a stock's quality. Under no circumstances should these rankings be regarded as a recommendation to buy or sell a security."

After the above caveat, they go on to explain that they "examine the earnings record of the past eight years. In measuring earnings stability, a basic score is given for each year in which net per share equals or exceeds that of the preceding year. For any year in which earnings declined, the score is reduced by the percentage of that decline. The average of these eight annual scores, weighted for frequency of earnings declines, becomes our first 'basic earnings index'!"

There is a further explanation, but that is the general idea. Their filtering of hundreds of stocks in the S & P monthly stock summary, using each stock's earnings (and dividends) criteria, provides us with a wonderful initial screening. Since we are concerned also with the quality of earnings, it only makes sense to investigate further the companies that are grade "A" or better.

How To Buy "Grade A" Growth Companies

We will apply the usual requirements: that the earnings continue to be growing for the latest four years and four quarters.

HOW QUALITY WAS USED
AT THE BEGINNING OF THE BULL MARKET

Here's a table that was made up of many growth companies that came from just the A's and B's. If I went through the whole list I'd have filled a suburban phone book. And I don't want to bore you to death with too many examples. Their earnings continued to show persistent increases. Remember the time is the end of May, 1975, when the leading indicators gave a buy signal. The ratings for each stock came from the S & P monthly stock summary.

Stock	Grade	Close on 5/26/75	1976 High
Abbott Labs	A	35-3/4	55-1/4 (Had 2/1 split)
Albertson's	A	18	23-7/8
Am.Nat.Resources (was Am.Nat.Gas)	A	35-3/8	44-5/8
Anderson Clayton	A	14-1/8	25 (Had 2/1 split)
Bearings	A	22-1/2	31-3/4
Big Three	A	26-1/2	40-1/2 (Had 2/1 split)
Blue Bell	A	13-7/8	29-3/8 (Had 2/1 split)
Borden	A	24-3/8	34

How To Buy "Grade A" Growth Companies

As you can see this is only a small sampling, but large enough for you to see how easy this is to use.

HOW TO FIND THE QUALITY GROWTH COMPANIES

Let me repeat what you do in order to find these grade "A" companies. As soon as you get a bull market turn, start going through the "broker's bible," the Standard and Poor's Monthly Stock Guide.

Every broker worth his salt must have one. In fact, any clerk who works at the Trader's desk, where orders are sent to and from the exchanges, needs one as well as the secretary who sends out the "open orders." They need this book in order to make sure the stock symbol is correct because it's the stock symbol and not the name of the stock that is used to transmit the buys and sells on the listed exchanges. A mistaken symbol means that the wrong stock will be bought or sold. And with business the way it is, the brokerage houses want to keep their "error accounts" as low as possible.

Anyway, I've gone into some detail to show you that the S & P Stock Summary is very easy to get. Your broker may even have an extra one for you to keep. In any case, he can certainly get you one to use at his office. Don't ask him to do your homework for you, although the analysis would do him a world of good. He usually has his mind on other kinds of stocks.

It's a good idea to do this work at the brokerage house anyway, since you'll have the Standard & Poor's Stock

How To Buy "Grade A" Growth Companies

Reports handy.

The run-down on each stock in the Summary takes two pages. So that you don't get the data on the second page mixed up with the stock on the first page, all the lines are numbered. I'm looking at Lilly (Eli). The data covers two pages in the book and stretches horizontally from one page through the other. In order to keep the data aligned, Lilly is #10 on both pages. It is important to match these numbers.

The place to start, however, is not with the name of the company, but with the column called "Earnings & Dividend Ranking." Start at the beginning of the book and go right down this column. As soon as you hit an "A" or "A+" company, jump right over to the adjacent page. Dont hesitate to look at the name of the stock—it'll only slow you up. After matching the correct numbered lines, check the yearly trend in earnings. If any of the years are lower, drop it and start again in the ranking column.

If all the year's earnings are up, check the column "Interim Earnings." If these are down, forget the stock and go back to the ranking column. If each year's earnings are up and the interim earnings are higher, then reach for the Standard & Poor's Stock Report—the "tear sheet."

On the back are the yearly earnings. See that these have traveled up for the last 4 years. Remember, you have to begin with the 5th year back. Then flip to the front side and match the interim earnings. Keep in mind that a six or nine months' earnings from the Stock Summary can actually mask a lower quarter. So be careful to break the last four quarters down.

Since the analysis of companies is continual due to the

How To Buy "Grade A" Growth Companies

changes in their financial success, Standard & Poor's is always changing the rankings on some of them. After all, very few businesses can maintain a sales or earnings trend because of a great many unforeseen factors. The great success of Winnebago with their recreational vehicles tempted General Motors to enter the field. The fine record of Polaroid with its instant pictures brought Eastman Kodak into competing.

Then top management may be "stolen away," causing not only a vacuum in the company, but also new competition.

The economy may also go into a tailspin and that's also quite effective in harming a company.

Or the Federal or State governments may pass legislation that is harmful to profits. Anti-pollution laws have affected copper, coal and automobile companies.

A gung-ho product might lose favor with the public. An outfit like John's Bargain Stores made a living just from buying up loads of items that were "hot" and selling them at outstanding bargains.

FINDING NEW QUALITY GROWTH COMPANIES

In order to keep abreast of the changes in a company's ranking, all you have to do is refer to the Monthly Stock Guide again. Every month, near the front of the book, is a page with five headings: Name Changes, New Insertions, Listings Pending, Ranking/Ratings and New Exchange Listings. It's the Ranking/Ratings section we're interested in.

How To Buy "Grade A" Growth Companies

It is here that Standard & Poor's keep us up-to-date on its ranking changes. Sometimes they're decreased and sometimes increased. We're only interested in the improved rankings. Any betterment to "A" or "A+" demands an immediate investigation, for it is in this way that we will add new growth companies to our buy list.

This is a service your broker can supply. It only takes a fast glance at the table near the front of the book.

That's all there is to it. Pick all "A" to "A+" companies from the rankings. Check the growth in earnings on the opposite page of the Stock Guide. Double-check the growth in earnings on the tear sheet. You will then have a "grade A" growth company to milk for profits.

CHAPTER 12

ALTHOUGH THERE'S NO WARRANTY WHEN YOU BUY WARRANTS—
Sometimes They Warrant Your Buying Them

Staid old Ma Bell. The stock for widows and orphans, American Telephone, made a bombshell of an announcement early in 1970. The reason was usual enough. The biggest company in the U.S. needed billions of dollars for working capital. But when the financial package was described, the surprise part of the deal was that A.T.&T. would issue a debenture with warrants attached.

By using warrants, the conservative utility was adopting a device that conglomerates had used when they were gobbling up smaller firms. After all, a warrant is nothing more than a piece of paper that allows the holder to buy a share of common stock at a certain price. If the stock is selling below the warrant's price, as is often the case, the warrant is worthless.

Although There's No Warranty...

Even the conglomerate heads who issued plenty of them, along with many Wall Street cynics, have labeled them "funny money" and "Castro's pesos." In fact, Ma Bell, in the prospectus, admitted: "a warrant is more speculative than the related common stock."

So why did A.T.&T. do the unusual? It had become very difficult to move large bond issues in this time of tight money. In order to take the heat off of interest rates, it was decided to add a sweetener to the bonds to make them more attractive to pension funds, insurance companies and banks.

Even the New York Stock Exchange, which for fifty-seven years had refused to accept warrants (the Amex did a big business in them all along), decided to accept them.

By issuing the warrants, A.T.&T.'s treasurer, John Scanlon, figured his company reduced the interest rate on its debentures by a half-point. This would save his company $235 million over their thirty-year life. That's a lot of dimes, even for Ma Bell!

Beyond the saving of money, warrants offer the issuer another advantage. If the market slides, no one will exercise his warrants, so there will be no dilution at all. In fact, many warrants are never exercised. The best estimate is that about 80% of all warrants issued to date have traded until the day they died (that is, they were never converted into the common).

THE YO-YO CHARACTERISTICS OF WARRANTS

Warrants are the most volatile of speculations. They

Although There's No Warranty...

can be dazzling and dangerous. One financial magazine pointed out that the perpetual (no expiration date) Tri-Continental Corporation warrants, which had fallen to great lows in 1942, staged a spectacular come-back in the long market advance of the next twenty-five years. A $100 investment in them in 1942 would have been worth something over $220,000 by the time A.T.&T. had issued its warrants.

To show how dangerous warrants can be, here is a list of 1969 bear market prices.

	1969 Stk Prices			1969 Warrant Prices		
Company	High	Low	% Change	High	Low	% Change
AMK Corp.	55-1/4	21-1/8	-62%	18-1/8	6-1/8	-66%
Allegheny Air	29-5/8	10	-66%	21-1/2	5	-77%
Avco	49-5/8	22-1/2	-54%	13-3/8	5	-63%
Braniff	23-1/2	10	-57%	30-1/8	8	-73%
Indian Head	42-1/2	22-3/8	-47%	26	8-1/2	-67%
Lerner Stores	33-5/8	19-1/2	-42%	19-5/8	10-1/8	-48%
Trans Wrld Air.	48-3/4	21	-57%	34-1/4	10	-71%

Notice how much more the warrants sunk than the common. In fact, there is a technique used to take advantage of this phenomenon. It's called a "full warrant hedge" and works similar to the "full convertible bond hedge."

We needn't be concerned with this, though, because at this stage of the game, we're only going to consider taking long positions in warrants.

Although There's No Warranty...

A USEFUL ANALOGY

Let's see if I can make warrants more understandable by drawing an analogy. You've heard Robert Burns say "my love is like a red, red rose" or a comedian picture the "shine in her eyes is like the seat of a motorman's pants." Well, some things can't be described in any other way, so we'll try it with warrants.

Over the last few years many companies have issued "rain checks" to their customers. The idea was adopted from sporting events held in the open air. When weather prevented the affair from taking place, a "rain check" was given out so the patron could view the event when it was rescheduled. The same idea was applied to an advertised item. After going to the store for a $10 advertised article and the store had run out, they would give you a "rain check," allowing you to come back later to buy the advertised special.

Let's say you gave the store one dollar as a deposit for the $10 item. The sales slip, now worth $1 allows you to return within two weeks, with an additional $9, to buy the article for $10.

That sales slip, which is really the "rain check," can be likened to a warrant. The $10 article is similar to the conversion price of a common stock. And the two week purchasing time is like the specific time element during which the warrant can be exercised.

In other words, by handing over the 'rain check' (warrant that cost $1) plus another $9, within two weeks (the time period you can exercise the warrant), you can buy the $10 item (common stock).

Although There's No Warranty...

To go a step further, suppose that after telling a friend what a great $10 item this is, he takes a notion for it and offers you $3 for your 'rain check.' His offer to pay $2 more than it cost you is what causes the value of warrants to increase.

Does this make the subject a little clearer? Well, anyway, here's the actual story on warrants.

WHAT A WARRANT IS

A warrant is an option to buy a stated number of shares of stock at a certain price during a specified time. Thus, A.T.&T. warrants allowed you to buy one share of common at $52 a share up until May 15, 1975.

Usually, a warrant has a time limit, generally for some years. The A.T.&T. warrants expired on May 15, 1975. Sometimes there is no limit to the conversion into the common. Such warrants are "perpetual."

Warrants often become valuable after they are issued. This value depends not only on whether the issuing company makes money and its common appreciates in price, but also on the price at which the warrant can be exercised. A market for the warrants comes into existence and the original owners can sell them.

Warrants are highly leveraged, due to the fact that they are a substitute for margin buying of stock—without having to pay interest or meet a possible margin call. It is this feature that I want to stress later on.

The holder of warrants has no direct equity in a company, has no voting rights and receives no dividends.

Although There's No Warranty...

HOW THE PRICE OF A WARRANT IS SET

How are the prices of warrants figured out? When the price of a common stock with a warrant is *below* the price at which the warrant could be exchanged for the common, the warrant is actually worthless. Being "below water," the warrant has only "speculative value." It's worth whatever speculators are willing to pay for the possibility that the stock will, sometime in the future, rise to the exercise price.

Whenever the price of a stock with a warrant rises *above* its conversion price, the warrant then acquires some real value. Where one warrant buys one share of stock, this value is simply the difference between the current price of the stock and the conversion price.

For example, at the end of September, 1971, A.T.&T. common sold for 43 and the warrant 8-1/8. The warrant really wasn't worth anything except its "speculative value." Why would someone buy one warrant at 8-1/8 and pay another $52 to buy one share of common at $43? In other words, he would have paid $60-1/8 for a stock that he could buy for only $43. It's not worth it!

Where a warrant entitles you to buy *more* than one share of its common, here's how you figure the conversion parity price,. Multiply *both* the price of the stock and the option purchase price by the number of shares which the warrant can buy—*before* you make the indicated subtraction. Here's the formula:

1. Multiply the number of shares which the warrant can buy by the price of the stock.
2. Multiply the number of shares which the warrant can

Although There's No Warranty...

buy by the option purchase price.

3. Subtract #2 from #1.

For example, Braniff Airway warrants enables the owner to buy 3.18 shares of the common if he gives one warrant plus $73. Braniff common at the time is $14.

Step 1: 3.18 times 14 = 44.52
Step 2: 3.18 times 73 = 232.14
Step 3: 44.52 minus 232.14 = neg. 187.62

The negative $187.62 means that the warrant is far under water. The price of the warrants was 15-1/2. That 15-1/2 is all "speculative value."

Any difference between the actual price of a warrant and its conversion price is speculative value, or the "premium." The premium will be larger if the holders of the related stock are optimistic.

How do you estimate the speculative potentials of a warrant? The great possibility for capital gains by using warrants is mostly a matter of simple arithmetic. Take a stock and its warrant where the conversion ratio is 1 to 1. Once the stock is selling at or above the option purchase price, then every 1-point advance of the common will be matched by a 1-point advance in the conversion parity price of the warrant. Since the warrant sells for less than the stock, *the percentage gain is therefore much larger for the conversion parity price of the warrant than for the stock.* (On the other side of the coin, the percentage loss is much larger if the stock declines. Just go back over the example given earlier of the bear market of '69).

Although There's No Warranty...

ONLY TWO RULES
ARE NEEDED TO BUY WARRANTS

The first use of a warrant that interests us is in buying long. There are only a couple of rules to keep in mind.

1. Buy only the warrants of a common stock that you would buy anyway. If one of our growth stocks has such a warrant, by all means buy the warrant. You will soon see how to squeeze more mileage out of your money.

2. Be very careful to buy warrants that will not expire shortly. Leave at least a two year span before they expire. About one year before they die, speculators will be putting on a "short warrant hedge"—buying the common and shorting the equivalent number of warrants. This helps to drive them down along with their natural tendency to decline in value as the expiration date approaches. After expiration, a warrant has no value—no matter how high the common sells for.

With these preliminaries over, we'll buy warrants. They were the Gulf and Western warrants that are traded on the N.Y.S.E. Gulf and Western common was also traded on the same exchange—and still is for that matter. The four years' earnings and the four corresponding quarters met our earnings criteria.

The terms of the Gulf and Western warrants were these: they expire January 31, 1978, and one warrant plus $53.55 would have allowed you to buy 1.75 (one and three quarters) shares of common.

The price of the common was 34-1/4 and the price of the warrant was 4-3/4.

Since the warrant entitled you to buy more than one

Although There's No Warranty

share of common, we'll find out if it has any intrinsic value (real worth) or if it is all speculative value, like the warrants given in the example about Braniff.

Step 1: 1.75 times 34-1/4 = 59.94
Step 2: 1.75 times 53.55 = 93.71
Step 3: 59.94 minus 93.71 = neg. 33.77

This shows that the warrants have only speculative value—just like Braniff's. Nevertheless, if we think the stock will move up we can buy the warrants.

Here's how you can squeeze more mileage out of your money (this is called leverage). If you bought 100 shares of common at 34-1/4, your total outlay was $3425. Instead of buying 100 shares of common, you'd use that $3425 to buy as many warrants as you could. How many warrants could you buy? Just divide $3425 by 4-3/4, the price of the warrant. This would have given you 720 warrants. That's a lot of leverage!

While holding the common, there was a two for one split and a ten percent stock dividend. The warrants were also split two for one. If you had owned both, you would have ended up with 220 shares of common and 1440 shares of warrants.

The high during 1976 for the common was 21-1/2. This price was not lower than our buy at 34-1/4, because it reflects the two for one stock split as well as the ten percent stock dividend. Suppose you had bought both the common and the warrants and sold them both out at the high, how would you have made out?

Although There's No Warranty...

COMMON
Sold 220 shares at $21-1/2 = $4730
Bought 100 shares at   34-1/4 =   3425 (subtract)
$1305 gross profit

WARRANTS
Sold 1440 warrants at $8-1/2 = $12240
Bought 720 warrants at   4-3/4 =   3425 (subtract)
$ 8815 gross profit

The warrants gained more than 575% on the common! The actual gain on the common was 38% as against the actual gain on the warrants which was 257%. That's some leverage!

Although there's no warranty when you buy warrants, sometimes they warrant your buying them.

CHAPTER 13

HOW TO TRADE SAFELY AND ALMOST FOR NOTHING

The little speculator is always complaining about the big speculator. The big "mahoffs" are the mutual funds, banks, pension funds, and the big block swingers. They save on commissions, receive inside information and have close contact with the makers and shakers of finance.

PROLOGUE OF
SOME SOPHISTICATED TECHNIQUES

But it doesn't have to be so. The small trader can be just as clever as his counterpart. All he has to do is to use the same techniques. This is the kind of dazzling footwork he can do with $5000 in cash.

1. He uses the same fundamental and technical analysis

another are common in the business world. Such options may be for the purchase of a piece of real estate or a house. When applied to the stock market, you would buy an option on a stock that you thought was going higher in price. This is called a call option because it allows you, at some definite future date, to call the shares away from the owner after which you can either sell on the open market or keep for higher prices. In this case it is also possible to sell your option to someone else at a higher price than you had paid. This, in turn, would give that second person the right to call the stock. The opposite type of option is a put option. Here you hope the price of the stock goes lower. At this time we are only interested in a call option.

By owning a call option, you control 100 shares of a particular stock for a limited time at a certain price.

In order to understand the nomenclature better, let's take a look at one we're interested in. Barron's has a section called *Options Trading*. All the options markets are listed there. We find ours under the Chicago Board Options Exchange:

		Sales (100s)	Open Int.	High	Low	Last	Net Chg.	Stock Close
Glf Wstn	Jan 35	85	344	6-1/4	5-1/4	5-1/2	-1/2	34-1/4

1. The name of the company is given first. Glf Wstn is the short-hand for Gulf and Western Corp.

2. *Jan* means that near the end of January, 1976, the option will terminate. The January option was chosen because, at the time, that was the furthest one out.

How To Trade Safely

Between the time you bought it and the third week of January, 1976, you will either have sold the call or will have exercised it. This is done by calling for the 100 shares of G.W. that you control through the call. The shares that you call can now be held for higher prices or they can be sold on the open market very soon after. A call would be exercised and the stock sold the next day if a good dividend is paid on the common, because the holder of the call does not receive the dividend, whereas the holder of the common does. So you exercise your call the day before the stock goes ex-dividend in order to get the dividend and then sell a day or two later.

3. *35* is the striking price and means that the seller of the call has agreed to deliver to you 100 shares of G.W. at $35 a share no matter how much higher (or lower) the stock goes. If G.W. is under 35, there's no point to calling the stock. But as G.W. travels over 35, the option will follow it. In an exuberant market, the option will even be worth more than its intrinsic value. The additional worth is the speculative value. Both together make up the price of the option, called the "premium."

For example, if G.W. is 33 and the Jan. 35 call is $1, that $1 is all speculative value. If G.W. is 35 and the premium is $1-1/2, that $1-1/2 is still all speculative value. If G.W. is 38, the premium should be no lower than $3 because that is its intrinsic value. The premium is likely to be more, say $3-3/4. The $3/4 is the speculative value because the $35 strike price and $3 brings the intrinsic value to $38, the price of the common.

4. Sales (100s) of *85* means that week 85 options were

traded.

5. An open interest of *344* means that from the beginning of trading in this option until this time a total of 344 are still being held.

6. The high of *6-1/4* was the highest the option traded for during the week.

7. The low of *5-1/4* was the lowest the option traded for during the week.

8. The *Last* price of 5-1/2 means the option closed at $5-1/2.

9. *Net Change* means that it was *down 1/2* for the week.

10. The *Stock Close* of 34-1/4 means that G.W. common closed at $34-1/4 for the week.

You can see that the 5-1/2 that the Jan/35 option closed at was all speculative value. This hefty premium meant that a lot of speculators were willing to pay through the nose for an option whose stock they were betting would go higher. (It did as we shall see).

DEEP DISCOUNT BONDS

Now let's talk about deep discount bonds. A bond is an I.O.U. on the company issuing it. It's just like a "marker" you give if you run short at the tables in Las Vegas and have to borrow money. A stock gives you a percentage of ownership in a company, whereas a bond does not. Since you're only loaning money to a company when you buy its bonds, you are given interest. This is the same idea behind putting money in a bank savings account. I might add that many times a stock holder also receives interest,

How To Trade Safely

called "dividends."

All stocks fluctuate in price. What you may not be aware of is that all bonds also have price changes. There are two major reasons for bonds to go up and down. The first concerns the earnings of the company. If the earnings are decreasing, the interest on the bonds may be forfeited. Even though the amount of interest never changes, that amount may not be paid until the company can do so either out of its earnings or eventually by bankruptcy and selling its assets.

The second major reason is the change in interest rates themselves. As interest rates in the general economy increase, the value of the bond will decrease. As interest rates decrease, the value of the bond will increase. Here's the reason why.

Suppose a few years ago you bought a bond for $1000 (par) and it paid you $40 a year. This came to 4% and was better than you could have received in a savings bank. But along came the 1970 credit crunch. Interest rates soared to over 8%. At this time, top rated bonds could have been bought at $1000 (par) that returned 7% to 11%, depending on the quality of the company.

If you needed money and had to sell your bond at this time, you would not have received your $1000. Instead, your bond would have decreased in value until its $40 coupon equalled the 8% yield that the current bonds were paying. For this to happen, you would have had to sell your bonds for $500. Here's the arithmetic of it:

$$40 \div .08 = \$500$$

How To Trade Safely

You would have lost $500 of your principal because your bond had to match the current rates of return. And your bond would be called a "deep discount" bond.

Now someone else who didn't need the money and could afford to wait until the bond reached maturity in order to receive the original $1000 would buy it. After all, he would be receiving 8% return on his $500 and could pick up a capital gain of $500 if he waited long enough.

The last point to consider when buying a deep discount bond is its safety. Two large companies rate corporate bonds, Moody's and Standard & Poor's.

Standard & Poor's grades bonds into nine ratings. Only the top four are acceptable, since these are regarded eligible for banks to invest in. The ratings are:

AAA - These bonds have the best degree of protection as to principal and interest. Their prices move with interest rates.

AA - These are the second highest quality bonds and differ very little from the AAA's.

A - These bonds are upper medium grade. They have considerable investment strength. Although their prices change with interest rates, they also are affected by changes in economic and trade conditions.

BBB - These are medium grade bonds. They're on the borderline between definitely sound obligations and those with some speculation. These bonds are more susceptible to down-turns in business and trade conditions than to investment rates. Most of the deep discount bonds that we're interested in will fall in this category.

What you are going to do is buy a few deep discount bonds with the cash you have left over after buying your call option.

THE "SHORT" SALE

The final idea to cover is the "short" sale. A short sale in the business world is quite common. Whenever a businessman sells something for future delivery, he has made a short sale. If you buy furniture for delivery in three months and give the dealer a deposit, he has made a short sale. After all, he has sold you something which he doesn't have. Your deposit is the binder. If the furniture costs him more than he had originally figured, then he makes less money. If he can buy it for less than he first thought, then he'll make more.

When you short a stock, you are in the same position as that furniture dealer. You are selling stock that you don't own, hoping to buy it for future delivery at a lower price than you originally sold it. (Compared to everyday business, there is much less shorting of stock).

The mechanics of making a short sale are as follows: Brokerage firms have margin accounts containing long stocks. The brokerage house must keep the shares, because the customers have borrowed money on them and the broker keeps the stock for collateral. Among the statements that are agreed to when these margin papers are signed is that any of the stock in the margin account can be borrowed.

That is the stock that the brokerage house borrows and which you sell when you short. Your sale goes to someone who wants to be long in the stock. He's not concerned who

How To Trade Safely

sells it to him. But the account that lends you stock needs that stock replaced at some time. This means that at some future date you will have to buy the stock from some seller in order to replace it. This is called "covering" the short.

In order to make a short sale, a special account, called a margin account, has to be opened. The exchange requires that you deposit at least $2000 cash or equities in this account. The amount needed for the short sale is 50% of the value of the stock. If you short a stock at $40, your $2000 cash should take care of it.

100 shares times $40 = $4000
50% of $4000 = $2000

So for your $2000, you can short any stock up to and including $40 a share.

One other mechanical detail is needed. In order to get off a short sale, the order has to be designated as a "short sale." It also cannot be gotten off in a falling market. This means that you need an up-tick in the price. For example, if the prices are 36, 35-7/8, 35-5/8, 35-5/8, 35-1/2, 35-3/8, 35-1/4, no short sale can be made. But if there is an up-tick like this: 36, 35-7/8, 35-5/8, 35-1/2, *35-5/8*, 35-1/2, 35-3/8, the up-tick at 35-5/8 will get a short sale off. Of course, you can always put an order in above the current market price. The first kind of order is called a market order, because you will have sold short on the first up-tick that the market in the stock has. The second kind of order is called a limit order because the price has to rally to a definite price before you want to get your short sale off.

How To Trade Safely

PUTTING IT ALL TO WORK

We received a bull market signal on the week ending May 26, 1975. The leading indicators gave a buy signal because they were up three months in a row.

What we are looking for is a call option on a growth stock that is bullish and that has a long time to go. Such a company was Gulf and Western (G.W.). The stock had already turned bullish and was on a small dip, which was just fine for buying purposes. The cost of the call was $5-1/2. This meant that any price over $5-1/2 was our profit (less commissions of course).

The next step was to buy some deep discount bonds for cash on the N.Y.S.E. It so happened that G.W. had such bonds. They were the 6's of 1988 and were selling for $650 (65). The rate of return on these straight industrial bonds was 9-1/4% ($60 return divided by $650 cost).

If you were starting with $5000 cash and had already paid $550 for the call, that would have left you with $4450 in cash. How many bonds were bought? Six bonds were bought ($4450 divided by $650 a bond) and there was money left over for commissions. The return from these six bonds after holding them a year equalled $360. If the $550 you put into the call option turned sour and you lost the whole speculation, the worst you would be out of pocket is $190 ($550 minus $360). The cost of your speculation would have come to less than 4% of your $5000 stake. *Now that's trading safely and almost for nothing!*

So far this is what we've done:

1. We bought a long term call option on G.W. Jan/35 at

How To Trade Safely

5-1/2.

2. We bought for cash six straight deep discount bonds on G.W. that will bring us back $360 by the end of the year.

3. The most we can lose (if the bond doesn't go down) is $190, or less than 4% of our $5000 capital.

At this point let's put our next "big shot" technique into play in order to see if we can increase our profits by a short sale.

If you look at the chart, Figure 16, of G. W. common you will see several points of interest:

1. You can see where the leading indicators turned bullish and where the stock had been bullish beforehand. This was at point "1," where the price exceeded the previous bulge by at least two points.

2. The arrows at the bottom of the page were the times the quarterly earnings came out. All were correspondingly higher.

3. There were two stock splits: the first was a two for one, the second was a five for four. Since we are only going to hold the call option through the third week of January, 1976, (because that is when it will run out), we have only to consider what happens to the option when the stock has a two for one split.

On September 1, 1975, G.W. was split 2/1. To compensate for this the striking price of the option was adjusted from 35 to 17-1/2. In other words, the striking price was cut in half. This gave us *two* calls for the one we had originally. So when we sell our call option, we have to remember to sell two of them.

4. Now let's get back to shorting. You can see some

FIGURE 16: Gulf and Western

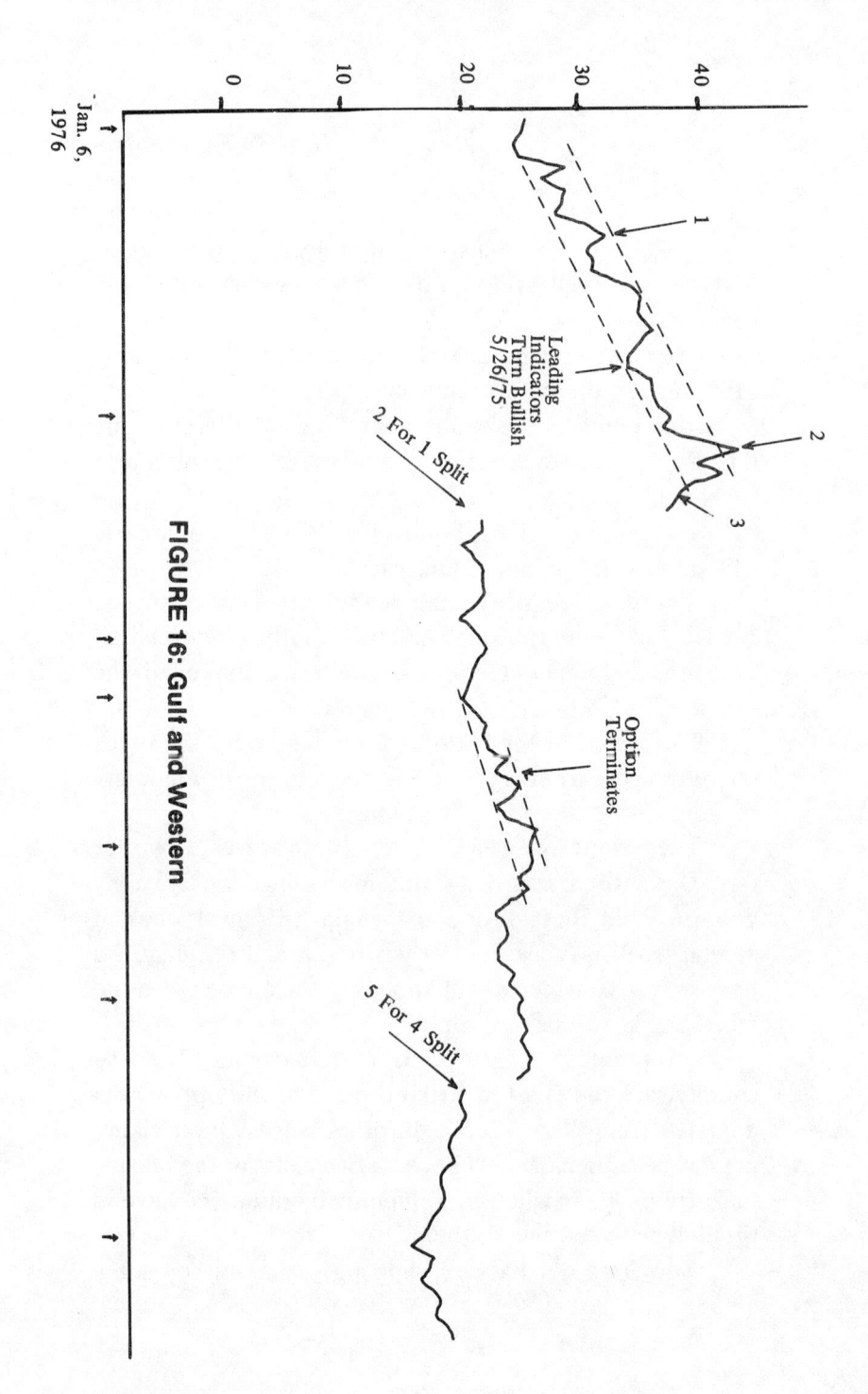

How To Trade Safely

dashed lines that run in "channels" or parallels. There is nothing fancy about this. It is normal for most stocks to trade up and down in channels until they change direction.

At point "2" the price became "overvalued" by breaking through the top of the channel. That's one place a short could be tried. The price the short was gotten off was 43-1/2. (Remember the bonds were moved into the margin account in order to provide collateral for the loan needed to short the stock). Our hope after shorting is for the stock to have a dip, but not a 20% one because that would knock us out of the box altogether. The place to "cover" the short is when the price pokes its nose through the bottom of the channel line and where it would become "undervalued." Four weeks later the price broke under the lower channel line and we bought in at 38-1/2 (point "3"). That's a profit of 5 points, or $500 more in our pocket for taking this *riskless* chance.

That's right. There was *no* way to lose any of our original capital on the short! The only loss we could have had was that we would not have made as much profit if the stock had gone higher than 43-1/2. How's that? What kind of verbal sleight-of-hand am I using? None...

After all, you do control 100 shares of stock with your call option. At the same time that you shorted you had a profit on your call, as you can see from the chart. If the stock keeps going higher, all you have to do is call for delivery of those 100 shares and use them to cover your short. So you've lost nothing, except that you have cut off the maximum capital gain you could have had.

In this case we won; our short was successful; we

How To Trade Safely

picked up an additional $500.

Let's unwind this whole bag of techniques that the sophisticates use and see how well we made out. The date was January 12, 1975, and the call is about to terminate.

1st.	Over the one year's time we received $360 interest on the straight bonds.	...$ 360
2nd.	The bonds were sold for 68-1/8 or $681.25. After $10 round-trip commissions, we netted very little, only $21.25 a bond or $127.50 as a capital gain.	...$ 127
3rd.	The call was sold for 5-1/2. (This was just a coincidence to our original purchase at 5-1/2). Since we now have two options because the stock split 2 for 1, then we have a gross profit of $1100. (We'll deduct $75 for the round-trip commissions).	...$1024
4th.	The $500 (less $75 round-trip commissions) on our short sale.	...$ 425
		$1937

That's 38% on our original capital of $5000.

There you have it—a perfectly legal but sophisticated way to trade the market safely and almost for nothing.

CHAPTER 14

THE "HAVE YOUR CAKE AND EAT IT TOO" SECURITY

ALL ABOUT CONVERTIBLE BONDS

There is an interesting hybrid security that can be bought. It's the "marriage" of a bond and a common stock, called a convertible bond. An owner of a convertible is somewhat schizophrenic. As a bondholder, he is a creditor of the company: whereas if he exchanges his bond for the common stock, he becomes a part owner.

The convertible bond has a specific maturity date when it will be paid off at face value and the debt wiped out. It is usually callable before it matures.

Conversion values of convertibles are protected, when stock splits or stock dividends are given, by having the conversion terms adjusted.

A company issues convertibles, or convertible pre-

The "Have Your Cake And Eat It Too" Security

ferreds, rather than common stock to raise fresh money for some very good reasons. Bond interest is 100% tax deductible, while dividends on both straight preferreds and common stock must be paid after all costs and corporate taxes. On top of this very important tax factor, continuing inflation works out well for the corporation selling the converts. You see, the money the company has to pay back will be worth less and therefore easier to acquire than the money they now borrow.

Convertibles are almost always issued at a price above their conversion parity. (More about this later). In effect, the company is really selling common stock at higher than current prices, and without presently diluting the stockholders' equity.

The money received from the converts is then used to increase the company's earnings. In turn, the better earnings should cause the common stock to rise in price above the conversion point for the bonds. This leads to some gradual conversion of the bonds. No shocks come as they would if all the bonds were converted at once and the earnings suddenly decreased because of the large amount of new common shares.

Finally, the company can save a good piece of change when interest rates are high. Since a straight bond issue must meet the competition from other high paying vehicles, the company can compete with the lower coupon on the bond by sweetening it up with the conversion feature.

To show that high rates of pay-out can have detrimental effects on the earnings of a company, witness this sample.

The "Have Your Cake And Eat It Too" Security

Occidental Petroleum reported its September quarter. It showed revenues of $1,037,000 as against a loss for the corresponding quarter of $11,461,000. These revenues did not lead to any earnings on the common shares, however, because the interest requirements for straight preferred exceeded the net income.

So instead of issuing straight bonds with a high interest rate, the corporation sells the convertibles. Some of the appeal of the common and some of the security of a straight bond are offered to the public. The corporation benefits by paying out a lot less interest than it would have to on a straight bond. The public benefits by receiving a higher return than it would if it had bought the common, and also participates in a capital gain if the stock moves up.

That's why a convertible bond should be bought instead of the common. The convert will appreciate together with the common, and also provide a higher return.

If you like the prospects of a company, check to see if there is a convertible bond. Almost always the convert will pay a higher return than the common. Keep in mind that only a small percentage of the thousands of public companies have converts.

WHERE TO FIND OUT IF A GROWTH COMPANY HAS A CONVERTIBLE

The best starting place is to look on the back of the Standard & Poor's Reports under the section called

The "Have Your Cake And Eat It Too" Security

"Capitalization." This will tell you all the kinds of equities the company has out. It will not, however, tell you where they are traded. There are only three places they can be bought and sold: on the NYSE, on the AMEX, or Over-The-Counter.

THE READING, WRITING AND ARITHMETIC OF CONVERTIBLES

Before we get into the guts of convertibles, let's look at one we were interested in at the turn of the market on May 26, 1975. This is how it looked in Barron's in the "Listed Bond Quotations" section.

1975			Sales	Weekly			Net
High	Low		$1000	High	Low	Last	Change
105	70	Alld St cv 4-1/2 81	4	105	103-1/2	104	+1

1. "cv is the shorthand for convertible. A bond without a "cv" after it is a straight bond. But don't get fooled. Some papers do a sloppy job on their typography and may leave the "cv" out, thereby giving you the false impression that there is no convertible. Even Barron's occassionally leaves out the "cv."

The only sure way is to look at the Standard and Poor's Bond Guide. The convertible bonds are listed in the back of the book.

Of course, there are advisory services that analyze converts—such as Standard and Poor's, Moody's, Value Line and R.H.M. Convertible Survey. Your broker or the

The "Have Your Cake And Eat It Too" Security

business section of a good library may have them.

2. "4-1/2" is the rate of return of the coupon. When Allied Stores' converts were first issued, they came out at $1000 a bond and paid 4-1/2%. This amounted to $45 for each $1000 bond.

3. The "81" is shorthand for the year the bond will "mature" or be paid off by the company. The "19" has been left out. So stick a "19" in front of the "81" and you can see that the year the bonds will be cashed in by the company is "1981." If the number is "04," just mentally slip a "20" in front and you come up with "2004."

Sometimes a company makes so much money that it wants to retire the bonds earlier than the maturity date. Because of the higher earnings, both the common stock and the converts have moved higher. You'll find the convert is way above its issue price of $1000. Let's say the convert is $1625 and the company says it will call them at $1006. (There will be an announcement ahead of time so don't panic). If you let the company buy them back for $1006, you'll lose a large capital gain. So you'll either sell the converts at the higher price on the open market or convert into the common shares, which you can then either sell or hold for higher prices. Experience has shown that you should sell your converts outright because the announcement causes the conversion of the bonds into more common and this, in turn, decreases the earnings per share.

4. The price of the bond itself is a shorthand number. The convert closed at 104. This does *not* mean $104; it means $1040. All the prices in the paper have been divided by 10. In order to restore the prices, you'll have to

The "Have Your Cake And Eat It Too" Security

multiply by 10.

5. During 1975, the highest price reached was $1050 (105 x 10) and the low was $700 (70 x 10). For the week, the highest price was also $1050 and the low was $1035 (103.5 x 10).

6. If there is a fraction with the whole number, here's the table you can use. We'll say the return will run between 5% and 6%.

```
    5's   = $50.00
    5-1/8's =  51.25
    5-1/4's =  52.50
    5-3/8's =  53.75
    5-1/2's =  55.00
    5-5/8's =  56.25
    5-3/4's =  57.50
    5-7/8's =  58.75
    6's   =  60.00
```

Now let's run through the prices of a bond below 100 ($1000).

```
    70    = $700.00
    70-1/8 =  701.25
    70-1/4 =  702.50
    70-3/8 =  703.75
    70-1/2 =  705.00
    70-5/8 =  706.25
    70-3/4 =  707.50
    70-7/8 =  708.75
    80    =  800.00
```

The "Have Your Cake And Eat It Too" Security

Finally, let's go through the prices when the convert is over par ($1000).

$$
\begin{aligned}
114 &= \$1140.00 \\
114\text{-}1/8 &= 1141.25 \\
114\text{-}1/4 &= 1142.50 \\
114\text{-}3/8 &= 1143.75 \\
114\text{-}1/2 &= 1145.00 \\
114\text{-}5/8 &= 1146.25 \\
114\text{-}3/4 &= 1147.50 \\
114\text{-}7/8 &= 1148.75 \\
115 &= 1150.00
\end{aligned}
$$

7. Four bonds were traded for the week.

In plain english, Allied Stores' convertibles paid $45 a year. The bonds, during the year, traded as low as $700 and as high as $1050. They closed near the high at $1040. The weekly high was $1050 and the weekly low was $1032.50. At the end of the week the bond was up $10 and four bonds had been traded.

FIGURING THE PREMIUM

Now that the basic terms have been cleared up, we'll find out if we're paying too much for the convert. This is called finding out the "premium," or how much the bond is selling above its conversion parity.

Remember that a convert gives its owner the right to exchange the bond into a fixed number of shares of common stock. This is called the conversion rate. Since

The "Have Your Cake And Eat It Too" Security

the privilege of converting is like a call option and since a 6 month call costs about 15% of the cash worth of the stock, then a convertible which sells for no more than 15% over the cash value of the stock it can be converted into is reasonably priced.

The only missing part now is: how many shares of common stock can you exchange the bond for? This information is not in the newspaper. It is most easily found in the Standard and Poor's Bond Guide. Allied Stores 4-1/2's of '81 could be converted into 35.7 shares of common.

Now here's all the data you need to figure the premium of the convert (or how much more the convert costs than buying the equivalent amount of common).

1. The convert closed at $1040.
2. The number of shares the bond converted into were 35.7.
3. The common closed at 30-3/8.

If we converted one bond into 35.7 shares of common stock selling at that time for 30-3/8, this was the stock value of that bond:

$$35.7 \text{ times } 30\text{-}3/8 = \$1084$$
The bond itself cost 104 or $1040.

This was an unusual case because there was no premium at all on the bond. In other words, there was no cost of a call option built into the price of the bond.

Since our premium rule (pay no more than 15%) was met, the bond was bought.

Another unusual situation showed up. The return on the

The "Have Your Cake And Eat It Too Security

common was 4.9% ($1.50 divided by 30-3/8) compared to 4.3% ($45 interest divided by $1040) for the bond. Almost always the return on the bond is higher than on the common. This is especially so with growth companies which are stingy payers in the first place, because they can make more money by ploughing it back into their own company.

The next question that comes up is: how many converts should you buy? Let's assume you are a 100 share buyer of the common, so that 100 times $30-3/8 (the price of the stock) equals $3037.50. The number of converts you could have bought for $3037 was 2.8 ($3037 divided by $1084, which was the price of the bond).

Since you can buy only even amounts, in this case 2 or 3 bonds, you will have to put up some additional money in order to buy three bonds.

The fundamentals of Allied Stores met our earnings' criteria for growth and the chart was set up. On the chart, the prices of just the common are used because the buy signal in the common will trigger the buy signal in the convert.

Before seeing how this technique worked out, there are a few general observations to be made. Firstly, the convertible definitely will move up or down with the common—like Joe E. Lewis and his shadow. There is not, however, an exact corresponding one-to-one relationship. Sometimes the converts lag a little, and once in awhile they will lead the common. But the discrepancy doesn't last long once the common has traveled up far enough to cause the bond to trade over par ($1000). On the way down under par, the difference sometimes widens enough to be taken

The "Have Your Cake And Eat It Too" Security

advantage of—but that's the topic of the chapter "Expect the Unexpected—Go Short of the Market While You're Long."

Secondly, although the price of the common is readjusted for a split in the price of the common, this is *not* so in the case of its convertible. It's the conversion rate that's adjusted. For example, if a stock splits two for one, the owner of the converts will be able to exchange the bonds for twice as many shares as before.

If you had bought 3 converts of Allied Stores 4-1/2's of '81 on May 26, 1975, they would have cost you $1040 (104) for *each* bond.

If you had sold them on Dec. 27, 1976, you would have received $1620 (162) back. That was a profit of $580 a bond, or 55%.

If you had bought the common for the same amount of cash, or $3120 (3 times $1040), you would have owned 102 shares at 30-3/8 a share. If you had sold the common for 46-5/8 (at the same time you sold the converts), you would have gotten back $4755 (102 times 46-5/8). This would have been a profit of 52%.

The profits were slightly better on the converts than on the common. The commissions, however, are considerably lower on the converts than on the common. In this case the in-and-out commissions on the bonds were only $30 whereas the round-trip commission for the common was $125.

Keep your eyes peeled for the convertible bonds of growth companies. Usually, the return is much greater than the dividend from the common. Because the bond

The "Have Your Cake And Eat It Too" Security

will move up with the common, you can have the best of these two worlds: the higher return from the bond and the capital gains from the price movement of the common.

CHAPTER 15

EXPECT THE UNEXPECTED— Go Short Of The Market While You're Long

HOW THE UNEXPECTED PAID OFF

Expect the unexpected! Not long ago, a man would shave with a double-edged razor. The opposite sides of the blade were the sharp cutting edges. Today, the double cutting edges have shown up on only one side of the blade, giving an even closer shave.

Some years ago many of us applied Noxema Skin Cream to our faces in order to alleviate sunburn. Then one summertime Lothario, who had a big date, needed a shave in a hurry. Forgetting he had just smeared Noxema cream on his sun-burnt face, he lathered up—and got the smoothest shave ever. Today, Noxema sells an additional line of shaving cream.

Expect The Unexpected

While Johannes Gutenberg was trying to figure out how to apply force to some portable type so it would leave its impression on paper, he became so frustrated that he took a vacation. He went to a nearby wine harvest. There he saw the power of the wine press as it squeezed the juice from the grapes. That's all he needed. He hurried home and invented the printing press.

Louis Pasteur, under the influence of his college teacher, took up the study of crystallography. Living things, such as a poppy or a dandelion, grow from a very small start to a form by which we can tell them from other living things. Many non-living things, such as table salt, sugar or ice can also grow from very small beginnings into shapes by which we can tell them from other substances. But their shapes are different from those of living beings. They consist of smooth, plane surfaces that meet in sharp edges and corners. These are called crystals and the study of them is called crystallography.

It was in this field that Pasteur made his first important discoveries which led to his brilliant germ theory.

He was studying his favorite mineral, Para-Tartrate, derived from the red Tartar deposits found in the vats of fermented wine. One day one of his Tartrate solutions became affected by a mold and spoiled. This kind of thing happens often in warm weather. The normal response of the chemist is to curse under his breath and pour the stuff down the drain. Instead, Pasteur reversed the process.

He turned his attention back to the spoiled mold and turned the "accident" into an "experiment" by studying the mold's action on the Tartrate. The result was, as Pasteur wrote, the first link in a chain of arguments which

Expect The Unexpected

led him into the study of fermentation, to the recognition that microorganisms play an essential role in nature, and eventually to his revolutionary discoveries in the field of infectious diseases.

It was Pasteur's expectation of the unexpected that led him to say that microorganisms could be changed from enemies into the allies of men. "In inferior organisms," he wrote, "still more than in the big animal and vegetable species, life hinders life."

This idea was finally carried out more than fifty years later, when penicillin was accidentally discovered. It started back in 1922, when Alex Fleming caught a cold. His nose was dripping and some of it fell into a dish at his laboratory. Doing what Pasteur did, he investigated the spoiled experiment instead of tossing it away. He found that his nose drippings killed off the bacteria in the mold.

Alex isolated the active agent in the mucous, which was also present in tears. It was lysozyme. But lysozyme was not very powerful as a germ killer. It took another seven years and another accident. This time the lab window was open and the wind blew in a spore of the mold penicillium notatum. The spore landed in a culture dish of staphylococci. But Fleming had been waiting for that stroke of luck for fifteen years. When the unexpected came he was waiting for it.

This reverse logic also applies to most other fields. In 1821, Faraday invented the electric motor. He even made a crude model of one. But for more than fifty years no one paid any attention to it. In 1831, he also invented the electric generator. A motor converts electric current into mechanical motion. A generator converts mechanical

Expect The Unexpected

motion into electrical current. It is hard to believe that the reciprocal nature of these two machines was not realized until 1873. By that time, huge generators were driven by steam power and made electricity. Faraday's earlier invention had long been forgotten. There simply were no electric motors.

In 1873, at an exhibition in Vienna, several generators were put on display. In the easy going manner of the Austrians, one of the technicians mistakenly connected a generator, driven by a steam engine, to a second generator which was standing at rest. The current fed into the resting dynamo immediately set it into motion. That is how the electric motor was born—completely unexpectedly.

APPLYING THE UNEXPECTED TO THE STOCK MARKET

There is also an unexpected technique that can be used in the stock market. In the previous chapter, you learned how to buy the convertible bonds of growth stocks instead of their common shares. The reasons were that the convertibles gave more downside safety, similar capital gains and a much better return than the common.

In order to determine whether you should have bought the convertible, you learned that the premium should have seldom been more than 15%. This simply means that you should hardly ever pay more than 15% more for the convertible than you would pay for the equivalent of the common. In fact, the best premium to pay was *no*

Expect The Unexpected

premium at all!

These two factors—a low premium and the ability to convert the bond into common shares—will allow us to stand the process on its head. By using these two elements, we will be able to do the most daring thing on the market—go short, and with practically no risk!

In order to understand this spectacular idea, you will have to climb into the shoes of Pasteur and Fleming and expect the unexpected.

WHY THE CONVERTIBLE BOND HEDGE WORKS

We know from the last chapter how to figure the premiums on convertibles. We know that often the premium between the convertible and the common narrows so that the premium becomes very small, less than 5%; sometimes it becomes zero. After this point only so many things can happen.

If the common moves up, the convertible will also follow it up. If the common advances enough, it will equal its conversion price. This is the price at which the bond can be directly converted into the common. If the common continues to advance in price, the convertible will move in almost a one-to-one relationship with its common. The premium will stay at zero, or within a small premium.

For instance, suppose that a bond was convertible into its common at $50 a share. As long as the common stays under $50, the convertible could sell at anything, from no premium to a high premium. But as soon as the common

Expect The Unexpected

hits $50 a share, there will be no premium, or a small one, on the convertible. In fact, this relationship will stay in effect no matter how much higher the common goes. The only time that the premium will widen a great deal is when the price of the common slips below its conversion price, in this case $50 a share.

As the common retreats further and further under $50, so will the convertible—but only up to a certain point. No matter how far the common falls, unless the company cannot pay the bond interest, there will be a floor beyond which the bond will not drop. This is its investment value, or what a comparable straight industrial bond will sell for that pays the same return and has the same rating. This widening of the premium is what we're counting on.

Let's say, in this case, that the stock falls 50% from $50 to $25. If the convertible were paying $50, or 5% when it was issued at $1000, and comparable straight industrial bonds are now paying 8%, then the bond should sink no lower than $625. At $625, the $50 payout on the bond would now equal the 8% payout on the comparable straight industrial bond. This is known as its investment value. The drop in the bond was from $1000 to $625, a percentage decrease of only 37-1/2%, compared to a 50% fall in the common. In this case, the difference between the sell-off of the common and the convertible is 12-1/2%.

Since in actual practice the convertible rarely falls to its investment value but settles at a higher figure, there is even a greater percentage difference between the common and its convertible.

Let's say that the convertible falls to only $700. This would be a percentage decrease of 30%. The difference

Expect The Unexpected

now between the stock's fall and the convertible has widened to 20%.

This 20% difference is simply another way of figuring the premium of the convertible over the common. *It is this premium that we want to take advantage of.*

Keep in mind the fact that you can convert your bonds into common stock. This also allows you to *short* the common stock into which your bond is convertible. That's right! It is the expected thing for you to buy the bonds and then to convert them into the common, where you'll simply be exchanging a long position in the convertible bonds into a similar long position in the common shares.

By inverting the process, you will maintain your long position in the bonds but will now *sell* the equivalent common shares. You will *not* convert your bonds, but will go *short* the equivalent common against your *long* position in the bonds.

Your objective is to wait for the *premium to widen* between the common and the convertible. If you buy the convertibles and, at the same time, short the common when there is a small premium, you make your profits when the price of the common falls *farther* than that of the convertible. At that point you unwind the process by converting your bonds into stock and delivering this stock in settlement of your short. That is, you return the stock you borrowed to make the short sale. The larger the difference, or as the pros say it, the larger the premium—the bigger your profits.

I know that this may seem as confusing as unraveling spaghetti, but try to expect the unexpected. Here is another explanation.

Expect The Unexpected

Suppose a common stock sells at $50. At this point, the convertible bond can be directly converted into the common. The premium on the bond now amounts to zero.

Suppose, further, that one bond converts into 20 shares of common. Five bonds, therefore, can be exchanged for 100 shares of stock.

At this point, you buy five convertible bonds. At the same time you short (sell) 100 shares of common. If the common goes up beyond the $50, so will the convertible. Since you are short the stock, the only way you can make money on the common is for the common to go down. But it doesn't. Every point it goes up, you'll lose $100. But this is offset by the equivalent rise in the price of the bonds. Since you're long the bonds, you make a profit. It's this profit that wipes out the loss on your short. For all practical purposes you have a fully hedged position that cannot lose any money. What you lose on the short side of the common is counterbalanced by the profits on the long side of the bonds.

At this point, suppose the latest earnings come out. They're down. The common starts backing off. So do the converts. But the common falls a little more than the bonds. The premium opens up to 5%.

The general market now weakens because of increased bombing, sending the common down some more. The stock falls further than the convert; the premium opens up to 12%.

Then the Wall Street Journal prints a negative article about the company in "Heard on the Street." The common gets trampled on as the funds stampede for the exits. The convert falls, but not at all as much as the common. Its

Expect The Unexpected

interest payout is now acting like a floor. The premium widens out to 35%. This is the time to unwind.

If some kind words are said about the company and some accumulation begins, the common will tend to move up more sharply than the convert. The premium narrows to 30%. When the premium narrows, so do your profits. And this is what we want to avoid.

So you unwind the "full convertible hedge" (for that's what it's called) by converting the bonds in stock and delivering the stock to "cover" your short sale.

The 35% premium is your profit, less the commissions.

By applying this twist to convertible bonds and the common shares they are converted into, you can short the market at virtually no risk. If the bond hedge does not work out, that is, if no premium develops between the convertible and its common, all you lose when you "unwind" is the commissions. This is certainly much better than carrying a straight short position, where a big rally can kill your pocketbook and give you the heebygeebies.

On the other hand, if the stock falls faster than the bonds, you have an opportunity to make some good profits painlessly. In fact, I have seen some premiums open up to over 200%. If you can catch one of these, you'll be a real hero.

MORE ABOUT A "SHORT" SALE

What I have in mind is something more modest, but profitable nonetheless. Before we take a look at Otis

Expect The Unexpected

Elevator. I want to explain what a short sale is in respect to the common of a convertible bond, since that is what half your strategy is going to be. There are a couple of differences between shorting on a straight position and using those of a convertible bond. I'll point these out as I go along.

Here's a simple case to illustrate a short sale. Let's say that you go to the butcher for your holiday turkey one month ahead of time. The butcher, not having a fresh turkey available, accepts your payment and tells you to pick it up three weeks later. The butcher has made a sale but could not deliver at this time. He is literally "shorting" the turkey. At some time in the future, he will have to buy that turkey to give to you. By buying the turkey, he is "covering" his short sale.

That is what you do when you go "short" the market. You sell stock that isn't yours, promising to buy that stock in the future in order to deliver it.

It's easy to "short" a stock. You just sign a margin agreement with your broker. Tucked away inside the agreement it says that you authorize the broker to lend themselves or others any securities held in your margin account. With the large number of margin accounts, almost any stock is available.

Brokers are happy to lend their customer's stocks, because this is the only way in which they can borrow 100 percent of the value. Banks don't give such terms. Sounds like Alice in Wonderland? Here's how it works.

You decide to sell Otis Elevator short at 47-3/4. To do this, you put up the regular margin, say 50%. Now your broker borrows Otis, either from another customer or

Expect The Unexpected

another broker. To do this he has to put up the value of the borrowed stock, 100 cents on the dollar. This is easy for him because he has already sold the stock through your short sale, and has collected the sales price. But whenever asked, he must "mark to the market," keeping the cash deposit equal to the value of the stock. Your monthly statement will show these "mark to the markets." Don't worry about them since they're only a bookkeeping entry.

If dividends are paid on Otis, you, the borrower, will have to make them good. After all, by borrowing the stock you created more certificates than the corporation had issued. Since the corporation is liable only for the stock it has issued, you have to make good on those extra shares. Actually, the stock is likely to open down on ex-dividend day to equal the amount of the dividend. So the payment of the dividend is not supposed to cost you anything. In any case, since the return on your converts is almost always higher than the dividend you have to pay out on the short, you're fully protected.

Let's set up a short sale on Otis Elevator so you can see what happens. Assume you covered at 23-1/2.

Shorting Otis Elevator

Short sale of 100 Otis at 47-3/4		$4775.00
Costs:		
Commission	72.00	
S.E.C. Fee	.20	
N.Y. State Transfer Tax	5.00	77.20
Net Proceeds		4697.80
Margin: 50% of net proceeds		
credited to account		2348.90
		7046.70

Expect The Unexpected

Short covering of 100 shares at 23-1/2	2350	
Less Commission	47	
	2303	2303.00
New Credit Balance		4743.70
Less Margin Deposited		2348.90
Net Profit on Short Sale		2394.80

A short sale, unlike the selling out of a long position, can only be made on an "up-tick." Suppose Otis sold at 48, then at 47-3/4, then at 47-1/2, then at 47-3/4. That last 47-3/4 is an "up-tick" and you can sell short there. You can also short if the next sale is also 47-3/4 or higher.

In the case of shorting the common shares of convertibles, everything holds except for the following.

The convertible bonds may be bought for either cash or margin. If bought on margin, this is usually 50% of the value of the bonds.

Once you're long the converts you can sell the equivalent amount of the common. This goes into a margined short account. But you do *not* have to put up any additional money.

Let's suppose you bought 5 converts at $1000 each. You could pay cash, $5000, or you could margin them at 50%, or $2500. (Remember you must meet the minimum $2000 requirement for a margin account). Let's also suppose that each bond converts into 20 shares of common. That allows you to short 100 shares (20 times 5 bonds). No additional money is needed. If the common is selling at $50, you will have shorted $5000 worth of stock.

Look at your leverage! If you buy the converts on margin and short the common, you are handling $10,000

Expect The Unexpected

worth of securities for only $2500.

EYE-OPENER ILLUSTRATIONS

Now we'll get down to the mat and do an actual full bond hedge using Otis Elevator. Otis met all the requirements for a growth company. Its last four years and latest four quarters earnings were up. These earnings were good enough to put the bond over par ($1000).

The premium between the convertible and the common closed rapidly, amounting to only 2.7% on the week we got our sell signal on the market (Oct., 1973). That met our first rule: Put on the full bond hedge when the premium is 5% or less.

This is how the premium was figured: one Otis bond was convertible into 21.51 = $1027 (Conversion value)

Market price of convertible = $1055
Conversion value = 1027 (subtract)
─────
28

28 divided by 1055 = 2.6% premium

At the end of October, 1973, the common was 47-3/4, the bond was $1055, and the premium was only 2.7%.

How many bonds do you buy and how many shares do you short? You have to start with the common because of the odd conversion rates. You short as close to 100 shares as possible and buy as many bonds as necessary to supply the stock.

One Otis bond converted into 21.51 shares. This is

Expect The Unexpected

about 21-1/2 shares per bond. Therefore, the purchase of 5 bonds allowed you to short 107 shares of common. You ended up fully hedged by being long 5 Otis converts at $1055 each and short 107 shares of common at 47-3/4.

Where do you unwind the hedge? This brings into play Rule 2: unwind the deal whenever the premium balloons to about 30%. Sometimes you'll get real lucky and have one work out quite handsomely and at other times you'll have to grab your profits when it gets close.

The week ending December, 1974, showed that the premium had widened way beyond the 30% level. It had actually hit 52%! The price of the common was 23-1/2 and of the convert $770. How much money was made?

The drop in the common was 24-1/4 points (from the 47-3/4 where the short was put out to the 23-1/2 where the short was covered). The profit was $2594.75 (107 shares times 24-1/4 points).

Since we were long the converts and they dropped along with the common, we lost $285 on each bond ($1055 minus $770) or a total on the five bonds of $1425.

Our net profit was $1169 ($2594 profit on the common less $1425 loss on the bonds).

Our original investment was $5275 ($1055 times 5 converts). Our net profit was $1169, or 22%. That's excellent on a riskless hedge.

DOUBLE YOUR PLEASURE—
DOUBLE YOUR PROFITS

You can increase your percentage of gain by doubling

Expect The Unexpected

the quantities—and all for the same money! Your original hedge was done with cash. This time we'll get all the mileage we can by using 50% margin.

Instead of 5 bonds, we'll buy 10 at $1055 each. Instead of shorting 107 shares of common, we'll short 214 shares.

Now let's look at the profits:

The profit on the common was $5188 (214 times 24-1/4 points).

The loss on the bonds was $2850 ($285 times 10 bonds).

The gross profit was $2338 or 44% on our original investment of $5275.

As you can see, everything was doubled, including your pleasure and profits.

We'll go through one more. This time it'll be the Macy's 4-1/4's of 1990 on a straight cash basis. It's probably occurred to some of you that this method doesn't depend on finding a growth company. A cyclical company will do just as well, because we want the common to fall as hard as possible.

Macy's crossed the $1000 threshold in October, 1973. Its bonds converted into 33.33 shares of common. The common closed at $29.

Three converts were bought for $1000 each, a total of $3000. One hundred shares were shorted at 29.

This convertible bond hedge was unwound at the end of December, 1974, when the premium reached 35%. The bond closed at $540 (54) and the common at 12.

The profit on the common was $1700 (17 points times 100 shares). The loss on the converts was $1380 ($460 a bond times 3 bonds). Therefore, the gross profit was $320, or 11% on your original capital of $3000.

Expect The Unexpected

Needless to say, if you had used 50% margin, you would have made 22%, or doubled your profits.

Here's a much more recent example of a convertible bond hedge. The year is 1977. Although the leading indicators are still bullish, this example shows what happens when a growth company starts to grow backwards. The shrinking earnings of Tesoro Petroleum finally became deficits in 1977.

Once again we put this hedge on when the convertible is selling over par (or $1000 a bond). On January 21, 1977, the stock sold at 17-3/8 and the convertible bond sold for 101 ($1010). Since the first rule is to put on the full bond hedge when the premium is 5% or less, we must check out the actual premium. This is how the premium was figured: one Tesoro bond was convertible into 59.17 shares.

59.17 x 17-3/8 (price of stock) = 1028 (Conversion value)
Market price of convertible   = 1010 (Subtract)
                              ─────
                                18

This was most fortunate. The bond had *no* premium. In fact it had a "negative" premium because you could buy one convertible for slightly less than the 59.17 shares of stock that the bond converted into.

So how many bonds do you buy and how many shares do you sell? Since you try to short as close to 100 shares (or multiples of 100) as possible, and since each bond allows you to short 59.17 shares, you can buy two bonds and short 118 shares.

Where do you unwind the hedge? This is where rule 2

Expect the Unexpected

comes into play: sell the bonds and buy the stock when the premium widens to about 30%.

The week ending Dec. 29, 1977, showed that the premium had ballooned to 58%! How much money was made at this level? The price of the common was 7-1/2 and the convert was 70-1/2.

The drop in the common was 9-7/8 points (from 17-3/8 where the short was put out to 7-1/2 where the short was covered). Since we were short 118 shares, we made $1165 (118 times 9-7/8). But we lost $610 on the drop in the bonds (2 bonds times $305 on each bond). Remember, two bonds were bought for $1010 and sold for $705.

The gross profit (without commissions) was $555 ($1165 minus $610). That's 27.5% on our money!

Of course, if you had doubled the amounts by using a margin account, you would have also doubled your percent of profits.

By turning the logic of the convertible bonds on its head, you can engage in the riskiest adventure of the market—going short! One Old Timer who shorted the market and never made any money at it, said: "Whenever you have lost the zest for food or sex, there's nothing like the excitement and stimulation of going short. I've never made much money out of it, but it certainly keeps me interested!"

By expecting the unexpeced, you should not only stay interested in the market, but also make a worry-free profit.

CHAPTER 16

THE TRACK OF THE BEAR—
Or How To Act
In A Down Market

So far, all of the material has been dovetailed to a bull market: the leading indicators, the analysis of earnings, and the "weekly minor trend" rule. But just as there are up markets, so are there bear markets. And we must learn not only how to recognize them, but to turn them into profits.

Oh, yes! Every bull market is followed by a bear market. The economy pulses in cycles. Almost all phenomena is cyclical—so why not the stock market?

THE CYCLICAL NATURE OF NATURE

Nature is full of these rhythms. You may recall that Joseph advised the Egyptians to store grain for the inevitable seven lean crop years that came after the fat ones. Modern studies have shown that there are long cycles at fairly regular intervals from extremes of heat and drought.

This cyclical weather pattern is due in turn to the "water cycle." When water is heated by the sun, it evaporates into water vapor. When the water vapor is cooled due to cold Polar winds, it condenses into liquid or solid water like frost, sleet, ice or snow. This endless succession of evaporation and condensation is the "water cycle."

Another example is the oxygen-carbon dioxide cycle. Green plants take carbon dioxide from the air and add oxygen to the air while making food, while animals do the opposite. We inhale oxygen from the air and exhale carbon dioxide into it. So these two major groups, the plants and animals, supply a substance that is absolutely necessary for each other.

Then there is the "life cycle." Every living thing has one. It starts life, grows to maturity, reproduces, grows old, and finally dies. Cells, too, have such a life cycle. They are formed, grow to maturity, make new cells, become old, and finally die. When plants and animals die, they decay. All the materials that made up their bodies change back into simpler compounds such as water, carbon dioxide, nitrogen, sulphur, phosphorous, and others. All of these substances are used again by other living things for building new protoplasm. Such is the "life cycle."

The Track Of The Bear

THE CYCLICAL NATURE OF MAN'S INSTITUTIONS

Mankind's social institutions appear to be cyclical. The rise and fall of countries may also be of such a nature. The economies of all countries are fine examples of the cyclical nature of human economic endeavor.

Arthur Burns, the presidential advisor, made himself famous through his studies of the cyclical nature of American business. In fact, it has only been through such intensive studies that the Government has been able to so manipulate the economy as to take some of the sting out of the peaks and troughs. No longer, so it seems, do we have major depressions, but only recessions and minirecessions. Nevertheless, we still have bear markets following bull markets, ad infinitum.

SIGNS OF THE END OF A BULL MARKET

It is, therefore, quite important to spot signs of the end of a bull market. First of all, the news is so bullish that a bear who speaks up is called dirty names. After all, who wants to be reminded that the party has to end?

Then, in order to temper an enthusiastic market, margin requirements are raised to 80%, 90% or even 100%. If you can borrow less money, you have to buy fewer shares. It's a way of snuffing off the fuel, because it's easy money that helps make the market roll.

Besides the margin requirements being raised, so are outside interest rates. The Government is raising the discount rate, the banks are increasing their prime rates, and corporate bonds are yielding much more than common stocks.

The insiders are unloading. We can tell this by the large number of secondary offerings and stock splits. A secondary looks good because it comes out at a price under the market high for the stock. You also can buy the secondary without paying commission. The sellers do this. You seem to be getting a bargain, but it's a subtle way of distributing the stock from strong hands to weak ones.

The same goes for a stock split. It's much easier to pedal a $100 stock at $25 after it's been split four for one. The public will much more likely buy 100 shares of stock at $25 than 25 shares at $100 a piece. When you see a lot of stock splits, start getting cautious.

The Dow Jones Averages are spurting. Practically day after day, these averages are spurting. So much so that there will be newspaper headlines or at least front page notices.

Finally, all your friends are talking about their sudden road to riches. Where have they been all their lives? Brokers are the most popular guests at parties. They're so busy at the office, you can't even get them to answer your call. Everybody is ready to buy his wife a fur, himself a Caddy, his family that Hawaiian vacation. Nobody's mad at anybody.

That is when you start to get skeptical. You may have heard that a skeptic is a person who, after smelling flowers, looks for the coffin. That should be you. It's your hard earned and hard won money that's at stake. Now's the time to keep those leading business indicators up to

The Track Of The Bear

date and catch the start of the bear market cycle with the "minor trend" rule.

USING THE SAME TECHNIQUES
TO GO SHORT IN A BEAR MARKET

If you will look at the chart of the leading indicators (shown in the second chapter), you will see that the "bear" market started after those indicators had turned down three months in a row. When this happens the government says that we are in a recession.

With the indicators predicting a worsening economy, not only should we sell out our long holdings but we should also go "short." To do this we simply reverse the whole process by looking for growth stocks that are starting to grow backwards. As soon as a flat or decreasing earnings report was spotted in Barron's, the chart of the stock was plotted in order to see where the "sell" signal should take place.

The leading indicators gave a "bear" signal on the end of October, 1973. Rite Aid gave its "sell" signal just two weeks after the leading indicators did. The high on the rally was 30-5/8. If we would ordinarily sell out a long if the price fell at least 20% from this bulge of 30-5/8, then we should by all means sell short when business conditions and earnings are in our favor. The 20% dip came when the price hit 24-1/2. So much for the timing of our "short."

What did the earnings look like? Rite Aid was a bona fide growth company in that its earnings marched

The Track Of The Bear

straight up from 1966 through 1972. Then later, in 1973 in the second quarter, the earnings started to turn a little soft. Here's the comparison:

	1972	1973	
1st quarter	.11	.19	(up)
2nd quarter	.22	.20	(down)
3rd quarter	.24	.23	(down)
4th quarter	.34	.18	(down)

As you can see from the chart, Figure 14, the lower earnings of the second quarter actually showed up before the leading indicators went sour, so we didn't even have to fish around for those poorer earnings to come out after the normal sell signal. We were all set to pounce on the poor stock as soon as everything else fell into place.

Where do we cover our short? Just the same way, only opposite, that we sold out our longs. We would cover the "shorts" if:

1. The leading indicators were up three months in a row, so as to give a "buy" signal; or...

2. The price of the stock breaks out over a previous rally point by at least $2 (this is the minor trend buy rule); or...

3. The earnings for any quarter turn up.

In this case, the first quarter monthly earnings came out in June of 1974. They were 21 cents, up from ten cents. This was over 100% and told us that Rite Aid was resuming its growth. This is the reason for buying in the stock at $5 a share. The profit was almost 80% (from 24-1/2 down to 5). That was a very handsome profit.

FIGURE 17: Rite Aid

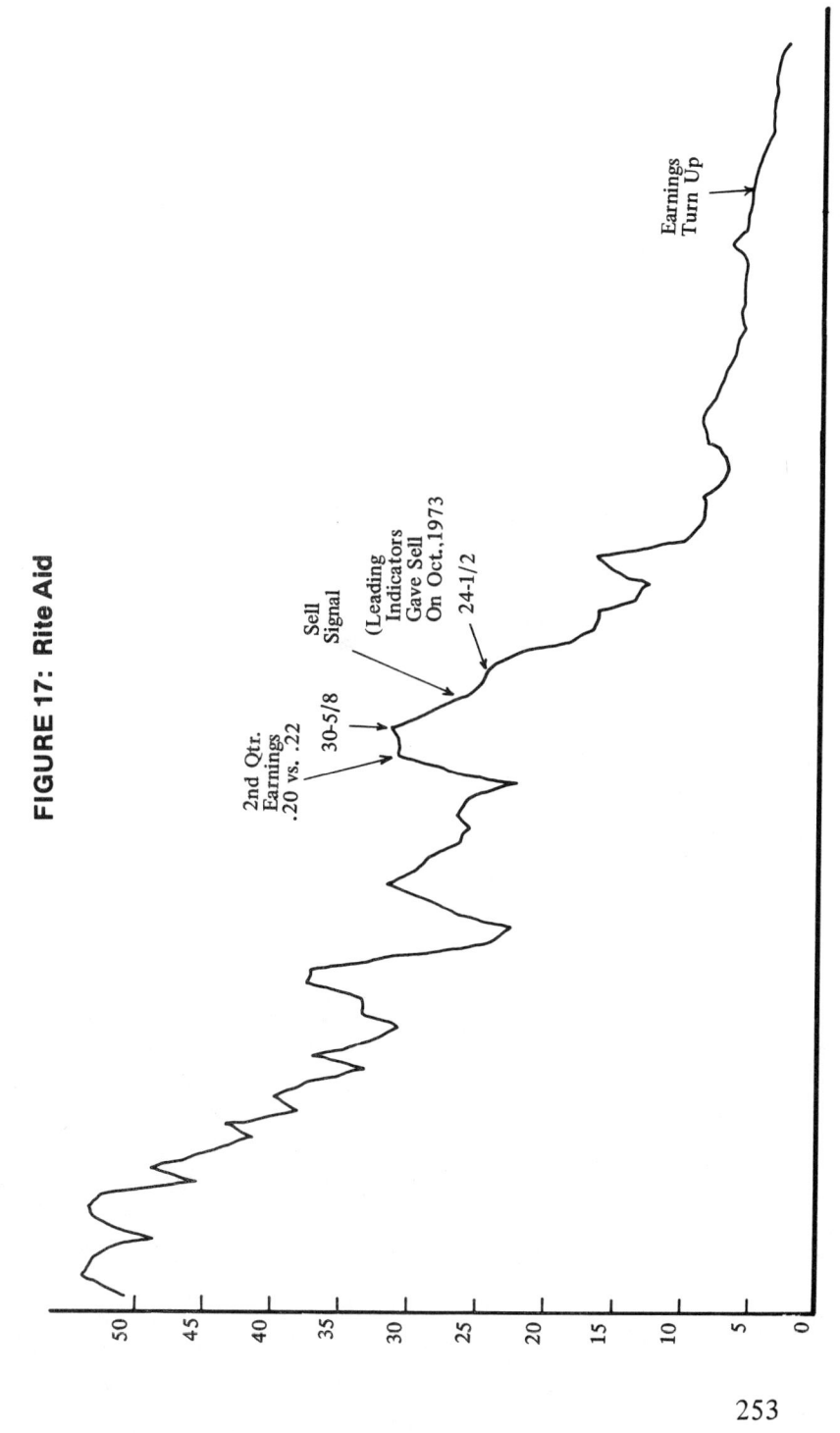

The Track Of The Bear

There you have it: a logical, consistent, easy-to-use stock technique that combines both fundamental and technical analysis in such a way that you should be a winner in both "bull" and "bear" cycles.

Good profits to you.